# BE YOUR OWN CFO

## A BUSINESSLIKE APPROACH TO YOUR PERSONAL FINANCES

---

George Grombacher

**Be Your Own CFO: A Businesslike Approach to Your Personal Finances**



While great efforts have been taken to provide accurate and current information regarding the covered material, George Grombacheris not responsible or any errors or omissions, or the results obtained from the use of this information.

The ideas, suggestions, general principles, and conclusions presented here are subject to local, state, and federal laws and regulations, and revisions of same, and are intended for informational purposes only. All information in this report is provided "as is" with no guarantee of completeness, accuracy, or timeliness regarding the results obtained from the use of this information and without warranty of any kind, express or implied, including, but not limited to, warranties of performance, merchantability, and fitness for a particular purpose. Your use of this information is at your own risk.

You assume full responsibility and risk of loss resulting from the use of this information. George Grombacher is not liable for any direct, special, indirect, incidental, consequential, or punitive damages or any other damages whatsoever, whether in an action based upon a statute, contract, tort (including, but not limited to negligence), or otherwise, relating to the use of this information.

In no event will George Grombacher, or his related partnerships or corporations, or the partners, agents, or employees of George Grombacher be liable to you or anyone else for any decision made or action taken in reliance on the information in this book or for any consequential, special, or similar damages, even if advised of the possibility of such damages.

George Grombacher is not engaged in rendering legal, accounting, or other professional services. If accounting, financial, legal, or tax advice is required, the services of a competent professional should be sought.

Facts and information in this book are believed to be accurate at the time of publication and may become outdated by marketplace changes or conditions, new or revised laws, or other circumstances. All figures and examples in this report are based on rates and assumptions no later in time than August 2022. Rates and assumptions are not guaranteed and may be subject to change. As in all assumptions and examples, individual results may vary based on a wide range of factors unique to each person's situation. All data provided in this book are to be used for informational purposes only. Any slights against individuals, companies, or organizations are unintentional.

# Contents

# Introduction

For over 20 years, I have been working as a financial advisor and helping people get better at managing their money so they can reach their financial goals and live how they want. I'm honored to be named to Investopedia's list of the top 100 financial advisors in the United States for many years running. Throughout my career, I've also spent a good amount of time training and mentoring other financial advisors so they can do a better job serving their clients.

I believe in taking a business-like approach to your personal finances. Accepting the responsibility of being your own Chief Financial Officer (CFO) will ultimately position you for personal financial success. If you want to get rich, that's what I want for you. If you want to stop worrying about money, I got you. If you want to live debt-free, I'm here for you.

I've been fortunate to have made a lot of great financial decisions in my life. Unfortunately, I've made a ton of bad financial decisions as well (which I will share with you throughout this book). Wherever you are, I'm confident I can help you get where you want to go.

## What Is a CFO?

Let's consult this CFO job description from the Society for Human Resource Management:

***Job Summary:***
The Chief Financial Officer will direct and oversee the financial activities of the corporation, direct the preparation of current financial reports and summaries, and create forecasts predicting future growth.

***Supervisory Responsibilities:***

- Oversees accounting department, budget preparation, and audit functions.

- Works with other department heads to monitor each department and make recommendations.

***Duties/Responsibilities:***

- Directs the preparation of all financial statements, including income statements, balance sheets, shareholder reports, tax returns, and governmental agency reports.
- Compares sales and profit projections to actual figures and budgeted expenses to actual expenses; makes or oversees any necessary adjustments to future projections and budgets.
- Reviews planning process and suggests improvements to current methods.
- Analyzes operations to identify areas in need of reorganization, downsizing, or elimination.
- Works with the President and other executives to coordinate planning and establish priorities for the planning process.
- Studies long-range economic trends and projects their impact on future growth in sales and market share.
- Identifies opportunities for expansion into new product areas.
- Oversees investment of funds and works with investment bankers to raise additional capital required for expansion.

***Required Skills/Abilities:***

- Excellent management and supervisory skills.
- Excellent analytical and organizational skills.
- Proficient in database and accounting computer application systems.
- Excellent written and verbal communication skills.

***Education and Experience:***

- Master's degree in business administration, accounting, or finance required.
- Certified Public Accountant designation preferred.
- Eight to ten years of experience in financial management required.

***Physical Requirements:***

- Prolonged periods sitting at a desk and working on a computer.
- Must be able to lift up to 15 pounds at times.
- Must be able to access various departments of a given location.

Over the next 20 chapters, I'm going to share with you what it will take for you to become your CFO. Let's get started.

# Chapter 1
# Your Financial Perspective

***CFO Best Practice**: The role of CFO has evolved from simply focusing on the books and records, compliance functions, and financials of an organization to being an indispensable member of the leadership team. Today's CFO must be adept at leadership, communication, strategy, and team building. They must be able to successfully support every aspect of the organization.*

Long ago, a traveler came upon a worksite where three stonecutters were working. Curious about what they were doing, the traveler approached the first stonecutter and asked, "Excuse me, sir. Can I ask you what you are doing?" The man glared up at her and said, "What does it look like I'm doing? I've got the worst job in the entire country. All I do is cut these stupid rocks all day. My hands hurt, my back hurts, my head hurts — everything hurts!" "I'm sorry for your trouble, I hope things turn around for you," said the traveler, and she moved onto the second stonecutter.

"Excuse me, sir. Can I ask what you are doing?" said the traveler. The second man looked up at her with a very serious expression and said, "I'm working to become the best stonecutter in the entire country." "That's an incredible goal, I wish you luck in achieving it," said the traveler, and she moved onto the third stonecutter.

As she got closer, she thought she heard the man whistling a cheerful tune. "Excuse me, sir. Can I ask what you are doing?" said the traveler. The man looked up with a gleam in his eye and said, "I'm building a cathedral."

Three men were doing the same work but had completely different experiences. How you look at something makes all the difference.

And this is true for every aspect of our lives, including money.

A positive financial perspective serves us well. A negative financial perspective can limit our ability to achieve our full financial potential. I'm going to help you explore your current perspective on money, and make any necessary changes.

My perspective on money has changed and evolved. This is true of my beliefs — how I think and feel about money and how I interact with money. One thing I know for sure is this — each of us can choose our financial perspective. Having a positive financial perspective sets us up for success. A negative one can limit our potential.

## What keeps us where we're at?

Inertia is "a property of matter by which it continues in its existing state of rest or uniform motion in a straight line unless that state is changed by an external force." We all remember Newton's first law of motion that states, "An object at rest stays at rest and an object in motion stays in motion with the same speed and the same direction unless acted upon by an unbalanced force."

What keeps human beings stuck? Specifically, what keeps us financially stuck? I think there are three forces at work:

1. An uncertain future
2. Everyday stress and anxiety
3. Historical shame

To break free and move towards a better future, let's unpack each of these.

### *An Uncertain Future*

Dealing with uncertainty is a cornerstone of the human experience. It's wisely said that we can't control the things that happen to us, but we can control how we respond to them. So much of our lives are uncertain: our health, the economy, and the stock market, to name a few.

If we're not comfortable and equipped to handle uncertainty in our lives, we procrastinate. When we procrastinate, no action is taken, nothing is created, and no progress is made. Because money has time value (the longer we wait to pursue our financial goals, the harder they are to reach), procrastination becomes a silent and slow killer of our financial objectives.

Learning to focus and take action on those things within our control is a key to overcoming uncertainty.

### *Everyday Stress and Anxiety*

We've all got a lot going on and feel like we're pulled in too many directions at the same time. There are many demands on our most important resources of time, attention, and money. It's easy to get overwhelmed.

When we feel overwhelmed, stress and anxiety creep into our lives. We feel like we should do more. When we're not able to do everything we think we should do, we feel guilty. These feelings can trap us in a vicious cycle that keeps us from pursuing our financial goals and objectives.

We break free from everyday stress and anxiety by accepting that we have limited resources and working to prioritize where those resources ought to be allocated

### *Historical Shame*

We've all done something dumb with money. But because money is still taboo for many of us, we don't talk about our struggles. Combine that with our perception that everyone else seems to do great with money, and our shame deepens.

It's a natural human emotion to feel shame about poor decisions. But, allowing that shame to prevent us from making positive moves is not healthy.

Moving past shame requires we address it head-on by owning any mistakes we've made, and moving past them.

## Recognizing our patterns

We follow predictable patterns, meaning we do things the way we do them, and others in our lives can be confident in knowing what we will do.

My morning routine is almost identical every day, as is my evening routine. My wife and I have very structured routines with our kids, which is good for them and us.

Human beings are creatures of habit. Many people love Monday Night Football, Taco Tuesday, and church on Sunday. Some of these people are productive and serve us, while others are negative and hurt us.

We also have habits and patterns we follow with how we handle money. Breakthroughs can happen when we realize our patterns and consciously work to nurture the good ones and get rid of the bad ones.

If you keep doing what you've always done, you are going to get what you've always got. Is there anything truer than that?

Einstein famously said, "Insanity is doing the same thing over and over and expecting different results." We have all been guilty of doing this. Why does this happen?

Our brains and bodies want to keep us safe. We crave the predictable. We crave patterns. To break free of patterns that are keeping us "safe," we need to identify our patterns.

What are your money habits? Spend some time thinking about your daily routines and habits.

- Aside from your essentials, are there things you are always spending money on? Are there things you refuse to spend money on?
- Why do you do the work you do? Is it out of necessity, or do you like it?
- Do you stay in career roles for certain amounts of time?
- What are your patterns around entrepreneurship, if any?
- Are you saving and investing money? Why do you make those savings and investing decisions?
- Are you a financial risk-taker?

What other money habits and patterns can you identify? It is important to recognize negative patterns and eliminate or replace them with positive ones.

## Checking your perspective

Recently, I read how a pair of Mahatma Gandhi's glasses sold at an auction for $340,000. While I don't have an opinion on whether that's the correct price, I wonder what the value of his perspective would be. Our perspectives are how we see the world. Fewer things are more important than that.

You and I look a lot different from outer space than we look in our bathroom mirrors.

That person on the internet that you think is overrated might look a lot more reasonable while sitting across the table from you at a coffee shop.

Everyone's perspective is real, but they vary widely from one person to another. One is not necessarily better than the other, but rather they're just different. When we recognize how our view of a situation or place can change, we can shift our thinking about it.

## A healthy perspective

"Whether you think you can, or you can't, you're right" — Henry Ford

Do you believe you can be financially successful? Is the stock market a place to make money, or is it a rigged game? Does money make people better, or is it the root of all evil?

Being able to look at yourself in the mirror and take an inventory of your life is key to a healthy perspective. Will you allow negative past events to define you, or are you a survivor?

You are someone who can be financially successful if you believe it. Combining the right perspective with a solid strategy can get you where you want to go with money.

**KEY TAKEAWAY**

The right perspective on personal finance can set you up for success while the wrong one can limit your potential.

**CALL TO ACTION**

Think and write about your current perspective on your personal finances. Is it helping you or hurting you? How can you shift your financial beliefs?

# Chapter 2
# The CFO of You

***CFO Best Practice**: According to Wikipedia, "The chief financial officer is an officer of a company or organization that is assigned the primary responsibility for managing the company's finances, including financial planning, management of financial risks, record-keeping, and financial reporting."*

*A CFO is the officer of a company or organization who handles financial affairs. This includes, but is not limited to:*

- *Financial planning*
- *Managing financial risk*
- *Record-keeping and reporting*
- *Data analysis*
- *Analyzing financial strengths and weaknesses*

*CFOs are top-level executives (often the third highest) who commonly hold a Master of Business Administration degree or a Chartered Financial Analyst designation, and/or have several years of experience in the accounting field or the financial industry.*

*Over time, CFOs have become integral members of the C-suite. They advise the CEO on strategy and help shape the vision and direction of the organization. As the financial authority, they handle accuracy and compliance with accepted accounting principles and financial standards.*

In an uncertain world, we crave control. We want to do everything we can to be physically, mentally, and emotionally healthy. And we want as much financial control as we can get.

What can you do to get more financial control? You can become your own CFO.

When you hear, "CFO" what comes to mind?

Do you think of a buttoned-up executive sitting in a corner office? Maybe you think of the brilliant investor, Warren Buffett. Or maybe you think about the great American entrepreneur, Peter LaFleur.

Peter rose to prominence from his portrayal in the movie DodgeBall: A True Underdog Story. If you recall, Peter was the owner of Average Joe's Gym. He was also the facilities manager, the human resources leader, and the CFO. We're introduced to Peter's love interest, Kate, when she shows up from the bank to audit Peter's financial records. We learn Peter doesn't have the firmest grip on his finances.

And what about you? How organized are your finances? Would you benefit from taking a more business-like approach to managing them? My goal is to help you better understand what a CFO does and how you can apply some of their best practices to your life. Doing so will help you get more financial control.

## What principles do CFOs follow?

An organization's current financial status plays and important role in all decision-making. Because of that, the financial data must be accurate and up to date. Therefore, the CFO needs to follow principles and processes.

This is done by following Generally Accepted Accounting Principles (GAAP). GAAP is a rules-based set of standards that includes 10 key principles. As companies grow, adherence to these principles becomes more important.

When a company goes public, its stock is traded on the markets and its financial statements must comply with the Securities and Exchange Commission (SEC). Following GAAP standards and principles helps position organizations for success.

## Be your own CFO

Imagine if Amazon or Google didn't follow GAAP principles or have great processes. Would they be as successful if they didn't track their cash flow or budget? Maybe, but certainly not as successful as they are.

Just as organizations benefit by following standards and having processes, you and I can as well. This book will guide you through everything you will need to become the CFO of you and take a business-like approach to your personal finances. The first step is accepting the title.

## Accepting the title

Will you accept the title of CFO? To gain more financial control, you need to accept personal responsibility for your money. You don't need to do everything, but you need to take an interest in every aspect. For example, you don't need to prepare and file your own taxes, but you need to make sure it gets done correctly and on time. This is true for every aspect of your financial life.

When we do these things, we give ourselves more financial control and position ourselves for long-term success.

## Our many roles and responsibilities

Have you ever heard the saying, "If you want something done, give it to a busy person?" Do you think it's true? We all wear many hats, and it's hard to get everything done.

I'm a husband, dad, financial advisor, podcaster, writer, short-order cook, dishwasher, housecleaner, and landscaper, to name a few. Like you, I've got a lot going on.

Because we all have finite resources, we need to be good stewards of them. We need to prioritize how we spend our time, attention, and money. If we're not being mindful of how we're allocating our resources, there's a long line of marketers who are interested in making those decisions for us.

It's important to me to find the right balance. One day, I will allocate those resources, spending 50% on work and 50% on the family. The day after that, I might spend 20% on work, 60% on family, and 20% on hobbies. The point is, my "balance" will rarely be the same two days in a row, and that's okay. My goal is to position myself for success and to do everything I can to allow my daily plans to survive their collision with reality.

We all know we have very little control over what life throws at us. The more intentional we are, the higher our chances of success.

## So many masters

In the Bible, Matthew 6:24 tells us, "No one can serve two masters."

It's easy to spread ourselves too thin and to over-commit ourselves. There are so many things I do today that weren't even an option 20 years ago, and I imagine that will be true 20 years from today. To protect our well-being, we need to increase our awareness of the things competing for our time, attention, and money.

There are so many things that exist today that weren't even an option 20 years ago, and I imagine that will be true 20 years from today. To protect our well-being, we need to increase our awareness of the things competing for our time, attention, and money.

These things may include:

- Social media
- Gaming
- The metaverse (web 3)
- Online betting
- Online trading
- Fantasy sports
- Subscription services (streaming)

Every one of these is consuming our time and attention. Many are also consuming our money.

I encourage you to make your own list of things you are spending your time, attention, and money on that you didn't use to.

## Being a good steward of our resources

We're all aware of social media algorithms, and we're becoming more aware of the value of our data. Social media has made us the product, and ads follow us around the internet, as well as between our devices. If we don't decide who we're going to give our resources to, there's an army of marketers standing ready to make those decisions on our behalf. So, we must become good stewards of our resources.

Would taking a business-like approach to your personal finances put you in a better place? If you were to implement more systems and processes, would you better position yourself for success? I think the answer is, "yes."

The more we can manage our financial lives like businesses, the better off we are.

## Being a professional

When you hear "professional" what comes to mind? I'm going to share four ideas that I believe make someone a professional.

***1. Becoming a lifelong learner***

Professionals are curious and always looking for ways to improve. Personal finance is a massive area and there's no shortage of things to learn. Embracing your inner student will help you better manage your finances.

***2. Doing what's required***

A true professional doesn't shy away from additional work. They don't say, "That's not in my job description." Instead, they go above and beyond and do what's required to complete the task. Because we're talking about your money, and your financial future, it's wise to adopt this attitude.

***3. Following through***

Professionals do what they say they're going to do. They follow through on things. You may be the head of your household and the only person managing the finances. Or, there may be several people handling the required tasks. Whatever your situation, it will benefit you to do the things you say you are going to do in a timely manner.

***4. Doing versus feeling***

A professional goes about their business regardless of whether they feel like it. You may never feel like reviewing your budget or preparing your taxes, but they need to get done. Putting your head down and getting the job done is a mark of a professional.

The more professional and businesslike we can be, the better positioned we will be to achieve our financial goals and objectives.

## Taking ownership

Finally, you need to take ownership of your personal finances. There will never be anyone more interested in your financial success than you are.

With great responsibility comes great power. As you take more ownership, you will grow more confident. As you grow more confident, you will take great interest. All of it will lead to positive habits, which will create constructive cycles. Nobody knows what the future holds, and we don't control what life will throw at us next. All we can do is position ourselves for success and let the chips fall where they may.

Taking a businesslike approach to our personal finances is a big step in the right direction.

**KEY TAKEAWAY**

Taking ownership of your personal finances will grow your confidence, create beneficial habits, and constructive cycles.

**CALL TO ACTION**

Think and write about how you can become a better steward of your resources.

# Chapter 3
# Your Personal Mission Statement

***CFO Best Practice**: Organizations have mission statements for many reasons. They want to give evidence to the world of why they exist and what others can expect from them. A mission statement communicates to its stakeholders, its customers, and to the general public what the company stands for and how they do business. The same is true for you and your personal mission statement.*

*When an organization strays from its mission, people can hold it accountable. Hopefully, this becomes an opportunity to course correct and make any necessary changes.*

*While the CFO's primary focus is on the company's financials, as a corporate officer, they also have responsibility for the overall success of the organization.*

There's a lot of value in having a personal mission statement. One major benefit is that it helps you prioritize your life.

Why is this important? Well, either you live by priority, or you live by pressure.

Have you ever known someone who's constantly running around like their hair is on fire or someone who's always five minutes late? I certainly have, and I have also been that person. We all have fallen victim to this phenomenon in our lives. The trick is not getting trapped in that frenetic lifestyle.

In my late 20s, I spent several years working with someone like that. This person seemed to always be playing from behind and trying to catch up. He never did. Ultimately, it cost him his health, career, and freedom.

While that's an extreme example, it's also a cautionary tale. We need to live by priority. Having a personal mission statement will help you do that.

### What is a personal mission statement?

A personal mission statement is a brief written statement. It articulates who you are, what you do, why and how you do what you do, and what impact you are aiming to have. It serves as the lens through which you view the world, and how you decide what to give your time, attention, and money to (and what to not). This simple written statement can help you navigate your life. It helps you prioritize.

### Why have a personal mission statement?

We have finite resources. The most valuable are time, attention, and money. Because they are finite, we need to be mindful of how we allocate them. If we're not making those decisions, someone or something else will.

As I mentioned, either we live by priority or we live by pressure. When living by priority, we can respond to situations as they come up mindfully, instead of simply reacting. What's the difference? If we are living based on priority, we come to conclusions after giving ourselves time and headspace to process those decisions.

When we use time and headspace, we take in information, consider various responses, and take the action. You've heard the term, "Sleep on it." When we take time to come to a decision, we make better decisions. The opposite is true when driving on a winter road, hitting a patch of ice, and having to immediately react.

When we don't have time and we are living under pressure, we are hitting ice patch after ice patch. Eventually, we are going to make the wrong choice and end up in a ditch.

I am constantly working to better prepare myself for everything that life throws at me. My personal mission statement is another tool that helps me do it.

## How to write your personal mission statement

As you are thinking about your mission statement, I really want you to get a pen and paper. The simple act of thinking and writing is a powerful combination that will help you successfully complete yours.

Start by thinking and writing about what is most important to you. Again, this is all about prioritization, so start big and narrow down your priorities.

Next, think and write about who you are now and who you want to be. I want your mission statement to be based on the ideal version of you, not who you are today. That doesn't mean you need to be that version of yourself every day — you just need to commit to striving to be that version of yourself.

Finally, think and write about how you like to do things.

Here's my personal mission statement: I help people get better at money so they can live how they want. I do that by encouraging, empowering, and delivering my message to them in an understandable way.

### How to live your personal mission statement

Put yourself on the hook. Share your mission statement with others. When you do this, you up the ante. You welcome others to hold you accountable for who you say you are.

Your personal mission statement is not something you do once and file away. When done correctly, it becomes a user's manual for your life. You can use it to decide on how you allocate your most valuable resources and how you respond to life's circumstances. It can be an invaluable tool.

I also encourage you to consistently (quarterly) review it. When your life and perspective change, you should update your mission statement accordingly.

## Stop living by pressure. Start living by priority.

There's immense value in living in alignment. You've heard the saying, "Stand for something or you will fall for anything." When you are clear on what your personal mission, values, and goals are, you know what you stand for and what you stand against. You have clarity around what is most important to you and what is not.

The opposite is living a life without principles, vision, or direction. It's following popular opinion and emotional whims.

Living in alignment means we're living by our top priorities. Our lives are full of tradeoffs — when we decide to do one thing, we forego another. Making those decisions based on our most important goals and values positions us for long-term success.

## What living in alignment means

We want to live significant lives and get the most out of the time we have.

Our most important resources of time, attention, and money are finite. When we decide to do one thing, we are deciding not to do something else. We are constantly making tradeoffs. When we live in alignment, our odds of making the correct decisions increase.

Living in alignment means having a personal (or family) mission statement and being crystal clear on your goals and values. Those things serve as your criteria for making decisions about how to spend your resources.

## The benefits of living in alignment

What does living in alignment do for you?

You optimize your life by making the best possible decisions. It's wise to weigh decisions based on what's most important to us.

When you live in alignment, it becomes easier to say "yes" and "no" to things. For example, when your budget is aligned, you know what you spend money on and what you don't. You may prioritize experiences over possessions, so you allocate your money accordingly.

The only way to live how you want is to know how you want to live. The more we can prioritize how we spend our time, attention, and money, the closer we get to living our best lives.

## How to live in alignment

You need to figure out what you believe in, tell the world by sharing your personal mission statement, and then testify every day through the choices you make.

## Setting expectations

Failing to establish expectations leads to problems. This is true in business, relationships, and every other area of life.

It may be a smart financial decision for you to work on Saturdays, but that decision could make your family upset. To avoid upsetting your family, talk about the greater benefit working on Saturday will bring to your family. Together, you can decide that you will work for four hours on Saturday morning and then spend the rest of the day together.

Again, life is a series of tradeoffs. When you do one thing, you can't do something else. In the previous example, deciding to pursue professional goals over time with family may be the best decision from your perspective, but you must talk it through with your loved ones.

When you do this, everyone gets on the same page. You avoid miscommunication and hurt feelings.

You want a significant life today and a significant life 40 years from now. As you are deciding and allocating resources, you will benefit from living in alignment. We will explorer how to set and keep your financial priorities in chapter 11.

**Key Takeaway**

Having a personal mission statement will help you live by priority instead of pressure.

**Call to Action**

Create your personal mission statement.

# Chapter 4
# Your Goals

---

> ***CFO Best Practice**: Businesses engage in a formal and organized goal-setting process. It involves strategic planning that takes into consideration time horizon, opportunity, and threats. This process demands constant updates.*
>
> *The CFO handles the finances of the organization, and they set goals and objectives for everything under their responsibility.*

Do you set goals? Do you follow a goal-setting process? The impact of setting goals is undeniable.

In 1979, recent grads from Harvard's MBA program completed a survey on goal setting, and here's what they found:

- 84% had no specific goals
- 13% had goals but they weren't written
- 3% had written goals and plans for accomplishing them

Twelve years later, the students were once again surveyed, and here are the findings:

- The 13% who had goals (but weren't written) were earning twice as much as the 84% without goals.

- The 3% who had written goals were earning ten times as much as the other 97% combined.

I've been aware of that research and the value of setting goals for a long time. But that doesn't mean I set goals.

Despite my knowledge, it took me until I was 35 to actually sit down and write my goals. Sure, I had goals for my business and fleeting ideas of what I wanted for my life. But I never put pen to paper to write my personal goals.

Today, I've been going through an organized goal-setting process for almost 10 years and it has had a profound impact on my life. I want to share it with you hoping it will have the same impact on your life.

## Goal setting overview

We, as humans, have many amazing superpowers. One of my clear favorites is our ability to create the future we desire. It is truly amazing if you think about it. When you take the time to reflect on what you want your future to look like, when you create a plan of action, and then execute that plan, almost any reality can be yours.

When thinking about goals, I like to focus on six key areas: family, community, money and career, well-being, personal development, and peace of mind.

I'm going to help you get clear on the future you desire. You will decide how you want to feel and think deeply about what you want. And you will set your goals and put plans in place to make them your reality. We will review the six key areas so that you will have greater clarity on what your future is going to look like.

## Word association exercise

"Once I get that new job, then I will be happy." "Once I get that car, then I will be happy." "Once I am married and have a family, then I will be happy." Do any of those sound familiar? We have an odd relationship with goals and happiness, and too often, we think about them the wrong way.

So, instead of thinking, "Once I get X, then I will be happy," decide how you want to feel, then think deeply about why you want what you want. Once you've done that, then you will set your goals.

I've found word association helps me to get clear on how I truly want to feel. For example, when I hear the words "good parent," I feel present, fully engaged, locked in, and focused. I have strong feelings about being a good parent. This is a clear priority for me.

When I hear "good neighbor" I have feelings of pride, commitment, and ownership. I have strong feelings about being a good neighbor. This is a clear priority for me.

When I hear "financial success," I feel comfort, security, and control. I have strong feelings about financial success. This is a clear priority for me.

When I hear "healthy," I think of feeling good, strong, rested, and having a clear head. I have strong feelings about being healthy. This is a clear priority for me.

When I hear "self-improvement" I get feelings of seriousness, importance, and commitment. I have strong feelings about self-improvement. This is a clear priority for me.

When I hear "contentment," I feel calm, relaxed, and at peace. I have strong feelings about feeling content. This is a clear priority for me.

Now, as you go through the prompts, you will resonate with some and not with others. That's the whole idea.

The exercise is designed to help you determine how you want to feel and set goals around making those feelings your reality.

For each of the six areas, read each prompt and write what comes to mind.

1. ***Family***
    - Happy family
    - Good sibling
    - Good significant other
    - Good Spouse
    - Good Child

2. ***Community***
    - Active member
    - Good friend
    - Stakeholder
    - Good neighbor

3. ***Money and Career***
    - Financial success
    - Debt-free
    - Investor
    - Successful
    - Wealthy
    - Good with money
    - A career you love
    - Dream job
    - Love your work

4. ***Well-being***
    - Healthy
    - Strong
    - Good foods
    - Exercise
    - The right amount of sleep
    - Stress-free

5. ***Personal Development***
    - Lifelong learner
    - Curious
    - Self-improvement

6. ***Peace of Mind***
    - Peace of mind
    - Contentment
    - One with the universe

I am certain that some of these prompts resonated for you and others did not. Review your notes and circle the one prompt that most stood out in each of the six areas.

## Five whys

Before we jump to what you want in each of the six areas, let's dig deeper and think about why you want what you want.

There's a lot of value and utility in asking "why." If you've ever been around little kids, you are familiar with how they use that question to dig deeper.

There's also a business improvement process known as "Six Sigma" that uses "why" as a means of problem-solving.

We're going to use it to dig down to the root of why you want what you want and to get really clear on what your priorities are.

Here's an example of how it works, using my desire to be a good dad.

1. Why do you want to be a good dad? Answer: I want this because I want to raise my sons to be self-sufficient.

2. Why do you want to raise self-sufficient sons? Answer: I want this because I want my sons to have good lives.

3. Why do you want your sons to have good lives? Answer: I want this because I want them to be happy and content.

4. Why do you want your sons to be happy and content? Answer: I want everyone to be happy and content.

5. Why do you want everyone to be happy and content? Answer: I want that because that would make the world a better place.

You can see that the second question is in response to the answer to the first question, the third question is in response to the second answer, and so on.

In each of the six key areas, pick at least one of your desires and put it through this framework.

This may be difficult, and you may have to think hard. However, the exercise is designed to help you really think about why you want what you want.

In the word association module, we focused on our feelings. The five whys focused on our thinking. In the next section, we're going to put them together and crystallize what your goals are in each of the six key areas.

## Goals Exercise

We all know how important goals are. We have all heard that having goals is essential and now know that writing them down dramatically increases our chances of achieving them.

So whether you are like me, or you've been in the habit of writing goals for a while, we are going to dig in and clarify and crystallize our goals. Let's get started.

The first area is family. Based on the work you did in the word association exercise and the five whys, what are your goals for your family life? Take all the time you need to write them down.

Our second area is community. What are your goals for your community life? Take all the time you need to write them down.

Our third area is money and career. What are your goals for your financial and work life? Take all the time you need to write them down.

Our fourth area is well-being. What are your goals for your physical and mental health? Take all the time you need to write them down.

Our fifth area is personal development. What are your goals for your growth and learning? Take all the time you need to write them down.

Finally, the last area is peace of mind. What are your goals for this important area of your life? Take all the time you need to write them down.

Next, let's apply the SMART acronym to each goal — **S**pecific, **M**easurable, **A**ttainable, **R**elevant, and **T**ime-based.

For example, if a goal is to lose weight, how do we apply the SMART framework?

Is losing weight specific? Yes.

Is it measurable? It can be and needs to be. Let's say I want to lose 20 pounds.

Is losing 20 pounds attainable for me? Yes, I believe it is.

Is losing 20 pounds relevant to my overall desire to be healthy? The answer is yes.

Is it time-based? I need to give myself a deadline to lose 20 pounds. Can I lose 20 pounds in three months? Yes, I believe I could.

So, instead of simply saying "I want to lose weight." I've given myself three months to lose 20 pounds. I have a lot more clarity around this goal.

So, apply this framework to each of your goals.

In our next section, we're going to get specific about how you are going to accomplish your goals and put a plan together for making them happen.

## Time horizon and action

It's important to be mindful of the time horizon when we are planning. We need to make sure our long-term goals like retirement are taken care of. We also need to have mid-term goals like funding our children's education and buying a home. And we need short-term goals like getting out of debt and taking vacations.

Once we've decided what we want to accomplish, I find it helpful to think about it in three-year increments. Why? Because, as human beings, we tend to dramatically overestimate what we can accomplish in one year and dramatically underestimate what we can accomplish in three years.

Think about it, it may be hard to become debt free in one year, but highly possible to do it in three years. The same goes for losing 100 pounds or starting a business.

What I'd like you to do is fast forward three years. Looking back over that period, what has to happen both personally and professionally for you to feel happy with your progress?

What are you most excited about?

What are you most worried or concerned about?

Finally, what's going to get you to that reality?

Take as much time as you need to answer these questions.

Yes, it's imperative to have long-term goals, but when we focus on the actions we can take over the short term, we set ourselves up for long-term success. Think about it like this: if you win the next three years, you will probably win the three years after that, and the three years after that.

Going back to your goals in the six areas, think about what actions you can and need to be taking now that will bring those goals to fruition. The SMART framework we went through will help guide you in this part of your planning process as you crystallize the actions and activities you need to take over the next three years.

Embracing goal setting will set you up for success — the results of the Harvard survey show that. If you are like I was (i.e., someone who knows the importance of it but isn't doing it), I implore you to take this seriously.

**KEY TAKEAWAY**

Properly setting goals can make a massive difference in your life.

**CALL TO ACTION**

Follow the steps and create your goals.

# Chapter 5
# Your Financial Facts

> ***CFO Best Practice**: A CFO stewards the assets of an organization, accessing and reducing risks, maintaining financial records, and optimizing finances. They must ensure the organization has a strong financial foundation and have a thorough understanding of all pertinent financial data.*

To become successful, you need a strong financial foundation.

As individuals, we go through three stages of our financial lives — protection, accumulation, and distribution.

During the protection stage, we set our foundation. In the accumulation stage, we save and invest for our short, mid, and long-term priorities. In the distribution stage, we take all the assets we've accumulated and turn them into retirement income.

To be successful, you must pay attention to the individual parts of each stage (insurance, investments, legal documents, etc.), and take an integrated approach to your planning. Getting organized and consistently monitoring our financial situation, as a CFO does, allows us to make any changes depending on what life throws at us.

## Your financial foundation

You've got to know your financial "facts." These are your beliefs about money, cash flow, budget, and credit. They make up a significant portion of your financial foundation. While I'm going to focus on these four elements, you must also have the proper insurance and legal documentation to solidify your foundation.

Over the next four chapters, we will explore each of these individually.

**KEY TAKEAWAY**

We go through three stages of our financial lives; protection, accumulation, and distribution.

**CALL TO ACTION**

Think and write about what stage of your financial life are you in (protection, accumulation, or distribution)?

# Chapter 6
# Beliefs About Money

***CFO Best Practice****: As the third-ranking officer in an organization, the CFO must embody and typify the company's mission and values. Every financial decision is made through the lens of that mission and those values. They must also encourage and empower others to do so as well.*

We all have an operating system, just like our phones. There are programs constantly running in the background, taking care of mindless tasks and making decisions on our behalf. Without it, we'd be in trouble because we make about 35,000 decisions every day. Our operating system takes care of the vast majority of them.

Where does it come from? Some of our beliefs were given to us through DNA and others are learned through our experiences as adults, but we downloaded the majority of them between birth and the age of seven.

What if it's not optimized, or we have limiting beliefs? Here's the good news — you can change them. It's possible to change the neuroplasticity of our brains and create new pathways or beliefs.

How do we know? The first step is recognizing any negative habits or behaviors. For me, it was not paying attention to cash flow, not budgeting, and waiting until the last minute to pay bills. Once you identify the behavior, work to trace it as far back as you can. Odds are, you will end up in your early childhood.

While we're talking about personal finance, we have beliefs about everything. The more you can recognize any limiting beliefs you may have, the better your chances of overcoming them. When you can replace limiting beliefs with positive ones, you've positioned yourself for far greater success.

Money has indeed been behind limitless stress and anxiety, and our pursuit of money commonly leads to burnout. But it's also responsible for tons of wonderful things and provides people with freedom, flexibility, and options.

If you feel like you are not good with money, it's my goal to help you change your thinking. That's because I don't see any practical value in feeling that way. I see only negative consequences.

## The danger of limiting beliefs

"Whether you think you can, or you think you can't — you're right." — Henry Ford

If you think you are bad with money, you are probably going to be bad with money. If you think you are going to be a bad swimmer, you are probably going to be a lousy swimmer. These are examples of self-fulfilling prophecies that happen when you act out a false belief and make it a reality.

How has thinking that you hate money benefited you?

How has it hurt you?

More importantly, where do you think that belief came from?

I grew up in northern Minnesota in a middle-class household, raised by a single mom who was a schoolteacher. There was never enough money.

Once a month, my mom would "pay bills." That meant she'd spend a Sunday afternoon with our household bills spread out all over the dining room table. This was an incredibly stressful time, and my brother and I knew to stay out of her way.

Because of this and other similar experiences, I developed a scarcity mindset around money, as well as a desire to avoid it. As a young adult, that manifested through not paying attention to my spending, not keeping a budget, living paycheck-to-paycheck, and being in and out of credit card debt.

## Changing negative beliefs to positive ones

Here's the good news — it's possible to rewire your brain. You can get rid of negative and limiting beliefs and replace them with positive ones.

Neuroplasticity is the brain's ability to change and adapt as a result of experience.

The trick is to pay attention to your behaviors and to notice yourself engaging in limiting or damaging behaviors. When you catch yourself, work to trace it back to the earliest experiences. The more you can notice and catch your behaviors, the faster you will be able to nip them in the bud.

One of the greatest human attributes is our ability to recognize when our thinking is flawed and our ability to change our minds.

Think critically about your thinking. What if the opposite of what you believe about money is true?

Now, I'm not saying you should start loving money. Rather, I'm advocating you start looking at it for what it is — a tool for helping you get what you want in life.

**KEY TAKEAWAY**

Identifying and eliminating limiting beliefs will increase your financial potential.

**CALL TO ACTION**

How do you know what your beliefs are about money? Fill in the blanks below without thinking too deeply about your answers:

- People with money are __________
- Money makes people __________
- I'd have more money if __________
- My parents thought money would __________
- In my family, money caused __________
- Money equals __________
- If I had money, I'd __________
- If I could afford it, I'd __________
- Money is __________
- Money causes __________
- Having money is not __________
- In order to have more money, I'd need to __________
- When I have money, I usually __________
- I think money __________
- People think money __________

# Chapter 7
# Understanding Your Cash Flow

***CFO Best Practice**: CFOs must manage uncertainty around cash flow and maintain enough liquidity to cover monthly overhead.*

*Cash flow is the total amount of money being transferred in and out of a business. When a company has consistent, positive cash flow, its liquid assets are increasing. This allows the CFO to make proactive financial decisions such as reinvesting in the business or returning money to shareholders.*

*Shareholder value is created by a company's ability to generate positive cash flow.*

*Revenue - Expenses = Profit. This simple formula is essential to the success of an organization.*

Have you ever run out of money? When was the last time it happened?

Credit has made running out of money more difficult. It has also given us the ability to continue spending even if we're broke. This does not lend itself well to sustainable financial success.

Over two-thirds of Americans are living paycheck-to-paycheck. Essentially, that means they're running out of money towards the end of every month. Breaking free of that vicious cycle requires planning.

For the first half of my 20s, that was me. I never paid attention to how much I was spending. This was before online banking, so the only way I knew if I had any money was when I went to an ATM. At the end of the transaction, it would give me a printout with my balance on it. If it said $100 or more, I felt rich. When it said $.08, not so much.

It took me until my late 20s before I stopped ignoring my finances and started paying attention. Unshockingly, that's when things improved.

Having a monthly cash flow plan is essential. Without understanding how much money you have coming in, and how much is going out, you won't be successful.

When it comes to personal cash flow… earnings minus spending equals savings.

When we have a positive "Savings" number, we have positive cash flow. This means that we are taking in more money than we are spending. This is important because it allows us to save and invest money.

When we have a negative "Savings" number, we have negative cash flow. This means that we are living paycheck-to-paycheck, and more than likely than not, we are stuck in debt. In that situation, we aren't able to save or invest and that keeps us from working toward our financial goals. Either you are treading water, or falling deeper into debt.

Gaining a better understanding of your monthly cash flow can help position you for success.

## Auditing your cash flow

A common saying in business circles is, "cash is king" and it's true. If a business isn't properly capitalized, it won't be able to continue operating. The CFO must ensure there's enough cash to cover all expenses. The same is true for you and me, so how do we do it?

Most people don't know how much money they earn or how much they spend. Do you?

It's easy to develop the bad habit of not looking at your finances. When we fear what we will find, we tend not to look. It's bad when we don't pay attention to how we are spending our money.

You audit your cash flow by logging into your financial accounts and reviewing your transactions. However long it's been since you last did this will determine how far back you must review. If it's been a year, look back over the last year's worth of transactions.

When you are not paying attention, things slip through the cracks. You end up paying for things you don't use, or that you no longer value enough to continue paying for. My wife and I fell into the trap of not paying attention to our finances early in our relationship. When we finally ripped off the bandaid and reviewed our cash flow, we found hundreds of dollars of monthly expenses we could easily get rid of.,

Look for things you can easily cut out and do it. If you are unsure about whether you want to get rid of something, take a couple of months off of it and see if you miss it. You can always add it back in later.

Break the bad habit of not paying attention and replace it by logging into every account you use to spend money at least once a month. This will help you stay on top of your cash flow.

**KEY TAKEAWAY**

It's essential to know how much money you have coming in and how much you have going out.

**CALL TO ACTION**

Audit of the last 12 months of your cash flow by logging into every account you use to spend money. Review every transaction. Are there any expenses you can eliminate?

# Chapter 8
# Your Personal Budget

***CFO Best Practice**: Without a budget, a company has no chance of being successful.*

*CFOs use budgeting to forecast and develop long-range strategies. They create annual budgets and review them quarterly. They track certain aspects daily.*

*What is a budget? It's simply a plan for our money. It helps us to prioritize how we're using one of our most important resources (money).*

*A budget is a tool that provides information on a business's financial situation. It's a plan for the future and a gauge of what's working and what needs to be changed. An effective budget tracks revenue, expenses, and profits. A good budget helps ensure a company doesn't overspend and lays the groundwork for how much it can reinvest for growth.*

*The CFO must systematize and automate the organization's budget as much as possible. Budgeting is more of a process than a one-time event and it must be updated as conditions change. As the financial leader, the CFO must focus on what matters most, and not waste resources on trivial matters that don't move the needle. They work to involve stakeholders at every level of the organization and communicate openly and honestly about the current financial state of the company.*

Just as I failed to pay attention to my cash flow in my 20s, I also didn't keep a budget. If I'm being honest, I still don't love budgeting, and my wife keeps ours. But I say with absolute certainty that budgeting is empowering. It tells us when we're on track to reach our goals and when we're behind. A budget will also tell you if you can afford to do things like go on vacation, donate to charity, or make an investment.

There are a lot of ways to budget, and none of them are right or wrong. The best budget for you is the one that you follow. You can use a paper document or a spreadsheet, and there are a lot of great apps and budgeting technologies available.

To help simplify your budget, I want to teach you the 50/30/20 budget guide. It's helped me and my clients get started with budgeting for many years.

The 50 stands for needs, the 30 for wants, and the 20 for financial priorities. Let's talk about how it works.

### Getting started

To start, you need to determine your after-tax income. This is almost as easy as simply totaling up the money that hits your checking account every month. Once you know that number, add in any employee benefit deductions that were taken out of your paycheck, like health insurance premiums, 401(k) contributions, and FSA/HSA contributions. This will be the number we're going to work from. For the sake of simplicity, let's assume that the number is $1,000.

### Needs

Needs are things you absolutely can't live without. Here are the most common items:

- Housing
- Food

- Transportation
- Medicine
- Insurance
- Child care
- Clothing
- Minimum monthly loan amounts, as well debt repayments

Based on our $1,000 monthly income, $500 (50%) should be allocated to your needs. Write all your needs and their monthly costs to determine if you are currently within the parameters.

## Wants

Wants are things that accentuate life. Here are the most common items:

- Subscriptions
- Travel and vacations
- Food away from home (Eating out and happy hours)
- Entertainment
- Designer clothing
- Designer accessories
- Fancy jewelry

There will be a fair amount of crossover between wants and needs. Clothing is a need, but designer clothing is a want. For example, the cost of a middle-of-the-road business suit may be $200 ("need"), but you may purchase one for $300 (The additional $100 would be a "want").

Based on our $1,000 example, $300 (30%) should be allocated to your wants. Write all your wants and their monthly costs to determine if you are currently within the parameters.

## Financial priorities

The final 20% of your budget should be allocated to your financial priorities. The most common items are:

- Debt repayments (contributions above the minimum required payment)
- Saving and investing

No one ever reached the retirement age and thought, "I wish I hadn't saved all this money." While there's no limit to how much you can save and invest, 20% is the number you should strive to achieve.

Based on our $1,000 example, $200 (20%) should be allocated to your financial priorities. Write all of yours and their monthly costs to determine if you are currently within the parameters.

When you are getting started with budgeting, you may find it to be restrictive or uncomfortable. Those are perfectly natural feelings. Stick with it and I'm confident you will have a similar experience to mine — feeling empowered and in control of your finances.

**KEY TAKEAWAY**

A budget is a plan for your money and an integral part of your personal financial success.

**CALL TO ACTION**

Create your 50/20/30 budget.

# Chapter 9
# Improving Your Credit

***CFO Best Practice**: Credit plays an integral role in the financial operations of a business, and the CFO oversees it. They are responsible for the profitability and working capital of the company. Some companies use more credit than others, and every company is mindful of the importance of maintaining a positive credit profile.*

Credit plays an important role in our lives. Poor credit can prevent us from living where we want, driving the vehicle we desire, or working at our employer of choice. It can also cost us a lot of money in higher interest rates on loans.

Credit cards have made it almost impossible for us to run out of money. We can keep spending and spending, and spending. That negative behavior keeps many of us trapped with the average American being burdened with some amount of credit card debt. We need to become better stewards of our credit.

## Understanding credit and your current situation

A credit score is a number from 300 to 850 that measures your creditworthiness — meaning your ability to pay back the money you borrow.

Banks want to lend money to people who are likely to pay them back. With that in mind, the cost to borrow money for someone with a credit score of 850 will be less expensive than the cost for someone with a credit score of 300.

A credit score above 700 is "good," and working to get a credit score of at least 620 is a wise initial goal because that will allow you to do things such as qualify for a conventional home loan.

As I mentioned, the better your score, the lower the cost of borrowing money.

To understand your current credit situation, there are a handful of things I want you to do which will help us later on.

- Get a copy of your credit report. You are legally entitled to a free copy every year from sites like AnnualCreditReport.com

- Figure out your credit score. You can contact your existing lenders (e.g., credit card companies, student loan providers, auto loan providers) to obtain this information.

- Get your personal budget together (if you don't currently keep a budget, it is past time to do so)

- Get a total accounting of all your existing financial accounts (e.g., credit cards, bank accounts, auto loans, home loans, investments, etc)

## What are the factors that go into my credit score?

Many factors go into your credit score

- History of bill payments (i.e., timeliness of payments)

- Number of credit accounts you possess

- Utilization of your credit (ie., how you use your credit)

- Length of ownership of your credit accounts

- Recent applications for new credit

- Negative credit history such as collections, foreclosure, or bankruptcy

Again, these are objective measures lenders use to determine how likely someone is to pay back the money they've borrowed.

## How do I improve my credit score?

There are a lot of ways to improve your score, some of which may seem obvious

- Properly use your credit and make all payments on time. If you are able, setting automatic payments can help ensure on-time payments.
- Reduce your utilization to 30% or less. If you have $10,000 of available credit, bring your balance to $3,000 or less.
- Pay off existing debt.
- Keep old accounts open.
- Reduce the number of new credit applications. If you must open new accounts, try to open them around the same time.

## How long does it take for my credit score to go up?

When you start properly using credit, your score can improve as quickly as three to six months.

Negative events like foreclosure, collections, or bankruptcy can stay on your report for seven to 10 years.

If you follow these steps, you will create a solid financial foundation to build on. As you are working on the areas you need to work on, be patient with yourself. This is a worthwhile endeavor that may take longer than you like.

**KEY TAKEAWAY**

Being a good steward of your credit makes you an attractive borrower and will save you money.

**CALL TO ACTION**

Review your credit report and know your credit score.

# Chapter 10
# Overhead and Profit

***CFO Best Practice**: When working to increase revenue, a CFO has many options available. They can work to increase current revenue streams by delivering additional value and increasing prices. They can also work to create additional streams of revenue by adding new product lines.*

Businesses and individuals alike are always interested in improving their bottom line. It can be accomplished in many ways, but focusing on decreasing overhead and increasing profit are excellent starting points.

For businesses, Revenue - Costs = Profit. For individuals, Earnings - Spending = Savings.

## Earn more, or live on less

Years ago, someone asked me, "Is it easier to earn more money, or to live on less?" What do you think?

What goes through your mind when you think about earning more money? Does the thought of it excite you, or does it terrify you? Maybe you've got the time, energy, and attention to devote towards earning more, or maybe you are completely tapped out.

What about living on less? If you are in a position where there's not enough money to go around, and you don't see a path to earning more money, your only option is to figure out how to live on less. I've never taken a vow of poverty, and I don't expect you to either. But you may need to make cuts to certain aspects of your lifestyle.

When considering cutting expenses by modifying your lifestyle, it's really important to take a comprehensive view of your life beyond just money. The idea is to create a vision for your future that's better than your current situation. When you can do that, it becomes a lot easier to make cuts and sacrifices. From my experience, making lifestyle cuts for the sake of making cuts isn't a sustainable solution. Having a goal in mind that you can achieve helps to make the cut more worthwhile and therefore palatable.

## How to increase revenue

For individuals, there are also a lot of options for making more money.

If you are in a career you love, how can you earn more? What's the path to a promotion or increase in pay? Is there a new certification or designation you can earn? What would make you more valuable to your organization?

If you are not in a career you love, what pivot can you make to make more money? Does it make sense to go back to school? Do you have an entrepreneurial idea you'd like to bring into the world?

Do you have extra time, attention, and energy? If yes, there are a multitude of ways to earn extra money online and offline. There are great websites that offer money-making opportunities that could be considered side hustles to allow you to bring in additional revenue. Should you decide this is a good option for you, please check your employment contract to ensure you don't get yourself in trouble.

How you handle increases in compensation throughout your career can also have a massive impact on your finances. If every time you received an increase in compensation (say 5%), you increased your retirement plan contribution and your lifestyle spending (2.5% to retirement and 2.5% to lifestyle), you'd be positioning yourself for long-term financial success.

While it would be ideal to start that strategy in your early 20s, it's prudent to start today if you haven't already done so.

## How to reduce overhead

Just as when trying to increase revenue, a CFO has a lot of options to reduce overhead. They can look to reduce fixed expenses like rent, technology costs, and marketing. And they might also have to consider right-sizing their workforce (i.e., laying off employees).

For individuals, it's important to review your cash flow and budget, and there are six areas I encourage you to focus on.

### ***1. Cash flow***

Most people don't know how much money they earn and how much they spend. To get a stronger handle on your cash flow, you've audited your previous 12 months of expenses. Did you find anything you can cut out?

### ***2. Budget***

Having a budget is essential for your financial success. It's simply a plan for your money. It helps you know when you are on track, and when you need to make adjustments. There's no right or wrong way to keep a budget. Paper, spreadsheets, and apps are all effective. The key is finding what's right for you. You completed your version of the 50/20/30 budget guide. Were you within the parameters?

### ***3. Debt***

If you are in credit card debt, it's the first thing you should address. Credit card debt burdens the average American, and the interest rates can be over 20%. Credit card debt can prevent us from pursuing our most important financial goals.

### ***4. Housing***

We overspend on our homes and apartments. Your total housing costs shouldn't be over 30% of your gross monthly earnings. If you find you are over that number, it's time to make a change.

***5. Vehicles***

Vehicle expenses shouldn't be over 20% of your take-home pay. Just as with housing, if you are spending more than that, a change is needed.

***6. Food away from home***

Before the Covid-19 pandemic, Americans ate 50% of their meals away from home. That means buying food somewhere other than the grocery store. This is an easy trap to fall into but also an easy one to get out of. If you are in the habit of doing this, start changing your behavior a little at a time. If you are eating lunch out five days a week, start bringing lunch on one of those days.

If you decide to make cuts, I encourage you to think about them as short-term changes. Think of it as taking one step backward to take many steps forward. Any cuts you make will position you for long-term success. When you are on track to meet your most important objectives, you can always add back whatever you cut out.

What do you think? Will you pursue ways to earn more, live on less, or a combination of both?

**KEY TAKEAWAY**

Earnings - Spending = Savings.

**CALL TO ACTION**

How can you increase earnings, reduce spending, or a combination of both?

# Chapter 11
# Your Financial Priorities

---

> ***CFO Best Practice**: Because money touches every aspect of a business, a CFO must be ruthless with prioritization. Allocating financial resources to one part of the business means less or no resources to others.*

Because money plays such an important role in our lives, we must establish clear financial priorities.

While money won't bring us happiness, a lack of money can most certainly bring stress and anxiety. It's also really hard to think about the big picture and to plan our futures when we're drowning in debt, living paycheck-to-paycheck, and struggling to pay our monthly bills.

Taking a business-like approach to our personal finances will help us set and keep our financial priorities. When we take the time to get clear on what's important to us and create a structure around our personal finances, we position ourselves for long-term financial success.

If we're not clear on what's most important to use, we are at risk of making poor choices and squandering our resources.

Every choice we make has a consequence. When we choose to do one thing, we choose to not do something else. The better we can become at setting our financial priorities and following them, the better off we will be.

## Why have financial priorities?

We have a finite amount of money. And we all experience FOMO (fear of missing out), and we are all aware of YOLO (you only live once).

When we choose to do one thing, we choose to not do another. Money has time value, meaning the longer we wait to pursue a financial goal, the harder it becomes to achieve. Therefore, resources devoted anywhere other than our top priorities may be misallocated. That's why it's so important to decide what truly matters.

Setting and keeping your financial priorities will get you on the path to financial security, which will give you peace of mind. From there, you will be free to pursue financial prosperity — and that's ultimately what I want for you.

## Setting your financial priorities

To set your financial priorities, you need to get clear on your goals and values. Your goals are where you want to go, and your values will guide you on how you will get there.

When setting financial goals, I encourage you to think about them in terms of time horizon. Your short-term goals are what you want to accomplish over the next three years. Mid-term goals are what you want from three to 10 years from now. And, your long-term goals are what you'd like to accomplish 10+ years from now.

Once you've written them down, determine which are the three most important. From there, determine what actions you can take immediately to make progress toward achieving them.

Your values are the lens through which you see the world and provide a foundation for your decision-making. They help you make judgments and prioritize what to do and what not to do. Your values determine where you live, how you vote, and what you spend your money on. Therefore, clarifying yours is a worthwhile exercise.

## Aligning your finances to your priorities

The next step is looking at how you are currently using your money. The idea is to align your behavior with your priorities. To do that, you need to review your cash flow and your budget.

### Optimize your cash flow, spending, and budget

You've reviewed your cash flow, spending, and budget. I encourage you to consistently review these as your priorities continue changing. As your situation changes, there may be more opportunities to optimize these areas of your finances.

## Keeping your financial priorities

You know what your priorities are. Now it's a matter of honoring and following them. We do this both by focusing on what we want and by minimizing or eliminating what we don't want. You can put out a fire by pouring water on it, or by starving it of oxygen.

With priorities, you can eliminate things you are currently doing that aren't aligned (like eating out 7 days a week), and you can recognize when new things come up (like choosing to rent a more affordable Airbnb instead of staying in an expensive hotel). While it may not be possible to eliminate everything that isn't aligned with your priorities, we can work to minimize them as much as possible.

Using a cost benefit-analysis when making financial decisions will help you in this process. Here are the steps for completing one.

***Step 1***

Identify the project scope. Start by defining the question or problem you are trying to solve. We will use your summer vacation as an example.

Where will you go? Will you do a staycation, drive to another state, or travel internationally? What are the benefits you will receive? From there, you will take into consideration all the required resources.

***Step 2***

Determine the costs. There are four costs to take into consideration:

1. Direct Costs — Expenses directly related to your project (i.e, gas, plane tickets, hotels, food).

2. Indirect Costs — Fixed expenses (i.e., time away from work and potentially a decrease in income)

3. Intangible Costs — Costs difficult to measure directly (i.e., time away from school, extracurricular activities, a break in habits and routines).

4. Opportunity Costs — Costs of choosing one thing over another (i.e., a staycation will cost less money, but the benefits of experiencing international travel and different cultures are also valuable).

***Step 3***

Give each cost and benefit a dollar value. Create your full list of costs and benefits. While it is difficult to assign a dollar value to intangible costs, make your best estimate.

***Step 4***

Compare your findings. If the benefits outweigh the costs, you have a business case for moving forward. If they don't, you may decide to not pursue the project.

Using this straightforward process can help you decide if spending money on something makes sense or not.

Setting and keeping your financial priorities will go a long way in helping you find financial security and move toward financial prosperity.

Set and live by your priorities, and no one else's. You've got one opportunity at life, and we don't have time to waste. Get started.

**KEY TAKEAWAY**

Get clear on your priorities and use a process for financial decision-making.

**CALL TO ACTION**

Think and write about your financial priorities.

# Chapter 12
# Financial Planning

---

> ***CFO Best Practice**: Having the right strategy and planning are integral to the success of a business. The CEO works to set the organization's goals, decide on the markets, products and services to focus on, determine the competitive advantages, and establish systems and processes to create sustainable success.*
>
> *From there, the CFO determines if those goals are financially viable, where the biggest margins exist, the appropriate corporate structure, and how to track progress.*
>
> *To say there are a lot of moving parts would be an understatement.*

Taking a business-like approach to the financial planning process can help get you where you want to go with money.

The personal financial planning process also has a lot of moving parts. But it's not as difficult as people think. In fact, I think there's a lot of unnecessary complexity that prevents people from doing it. When we perceive something to be really hard, we don't do it.

## The benefits of a business-like approach

Thinking of yourself as the CFO of your financial life is a powerful thing. You will have clarity on your financial situation, have systems for reviewing it, hold consistent meetings to review, and know your most important priorities. It will help you to:

- Get quality data to make decisions. When you have accurate information, you will become more confident in your decision-making process while knowing that you are not guessing.

- Being organized will help you stay focused. When we're disorganized, it's easier to let financial matters slide and procrastinate.

- Improve communication with loved ones. You need to get on the same page when you talk about your finances.

- Prioritize how you spend your money. We have finite financial resources, so it's imperative we allocate them appropriately.

Would you be in a better financial position if you took a more business-like approach? I think the answer is "yes" for everyone.

**What is financial planning?**

I want to keep this as simple as possible.

Financial planning is determining your financial goals, looking at your current situation, and devising strategies for achieving those goals. It's best viewed as a process because it will need to be updated as your life changes.

The tangible result of a financial plan is a document that details your goals and the strategies for achieving them.

The purpose and value of financial planning and its fundamental goal is providing peace of mind knowing your affairs are in order.

You can create a financial plan for specific things like getting out of debt or saving for retirement. You can create a more comprehensive financial plan for your entire life. There's no right or wrong way to do it.

It's wise to think about financial planning as an ongoing process. You are never going to be "done" with it. As your life changes, your plan will also change.

Let's get into what the actual process is.

## Where you are

It's important to have a clear and accurate picture of your current assets, liabilities, legal documents, and insurance policies. It's also important to understand your risk tolerance, planning tolerance, and appetite for doing the planning. To get organized, gather any current statements, policies, and documents. Keeping a spreadsheet will also help you get and stay organized.

***Cash flow and budget***

You'll need clarity on your current income and expenses and your personal budget.

***Assets and liabilities***

This is a very cut-and-dry accounting of your current financial situation — what accounts and assets do you have, what is their value, and how much debt do you have. With this, you can determine your current net worth.

***Risk management***

Make sure you know the location of your existing insurance policies and legal documents.

***Planning tolerance***

This is your understanding of how you like to receive and process information. Do you prefer visuals or spreadsheets? Do you want all the details or a broad overview? This is important if you are going to be working with professionals; the process will be more effective if you are clear in your expectations and wants.

***Appetite for planning***

Are you ready to start this process? It will be time and attention intensive and you must be going to be fully engaged. We are, after all, talking about your money and your future.

**Where you want to be**

Without question, this is the most important part of the financial planning process — your vision for the future. You will need to think about what you want for your "future" self, your "future" family, and your "future" life. I put the future in quotations because it's difficult and abstract to think about ourselves getting older. But it's happening to all of us every single day.

Time horizon is a valuable tool in financial planning which we will dig deeper into in the next chapter.

## Closing the gap

We explored your current situation; you thought about where you will be in the future, and now it's time to close the gap. There are five key areas to address.

***1. Risk tolerance***

This is a measure of how comfortable you are with risk. How do you think and feel about market fluctuations? How do you think and feel about investing versus speculating?

It's important to take into consideration both your thoughts and your feelings because while we may intellectually understand something, we make a lot of our decisions emotionally and we need to be mindful of that. Your risk tolerance will dictate the investments and asset classes you use.

***2. Right coverages***

You will need to ensure you have the proper types and the proper amounts of insurance, including but not limited to health, life, disability, long-term care, and property and casualty.

***3. Right accounts***

There are a lot of different accounts to save and invest in. Selecting the proper account based on purpose, time horizon, and taxes is imperative.

***4. Right vehicles and asset classes***

From stocks to bonds, real estate, crypto assets, mutual funds, and commodities, there are a lot of vehicles available to save and invest in. Taking your preferences and other important variables into consideration, you will choose which to use to reach your goals.

***5. Right amounts***

Once you've decided on which accounts and vehicles to save and invest in, you will determine how much to contribute and for how long. You will run projections and make assumptions to ensure you are on track to meet your goals.

## Completing your plan

You've thought about where you are and where you want to go. You know your numbers and current situation. Now it's time to get it started.

As the CFO of your life, you are in charge. But that doesn't mean you need to do everything. There may be certain aspects you are interested in (like investing), and others that you have no interest in (like preparing and filing your taxes).

If you choose to engage with a professional, communicate that you value transparency and want to know all the fees and expenses that go along with their service. We will cover delegation in chapter 18.

**KEY TAKEAWAY**

You need a financial plan.

**CALL TO ACTION**

Determine which aspect of your financial planning you'll handle and which you'll outsource.

# Chapter 13
# Time Horizon

---

***CFO Best Practice**: Publicly traded companies must legally share progress reports quarterly. The CFO has a tough job because if the numbers they report don't meet expectations, the value of the company can be reduced. So, they are constantly monitoring today, as well as planning and deciding to make sure the company remains successful in the future.*

*Publicly traded companies are legally obligated to share financial information quarterly on a 10-Q form. There are unaudited financial statements. Annually, they must share audited financial statements and commentary from the management team on form 10-K. Because of these stringent requirements, the CFO must maintain detailed records.*

*More so than that, the CFO is responsible for the financial success of the company. It's their job to make sure all financial priorities are met in the short, mid, and long-term.*

*Publicly traded companies answer to their board of directors, shareholders, employees, Wall Street, and the media. When business and results are good, the job of a CFO is easier. The CFO must do a great job of communicating with all stakeholders. They must position their message and create a compelling vision for the future. When times are tough, we've got a plan for turning things around. When times are good, we're going to keep it going.*

Companies, sports franchises, politicians, and you and I all face pressure to deliver results today and into the future. We're all tasked with balancing today's priorities, needs, and wants with those that are longer term. Because of that, it's prudent to pay close attention to time horizon.

The Securities and Exchange Commission defines time horizon as, "Your time horizon is the number of months, years, or decades you need to invest to achieve your financial goal."

Money has time value. Meaning, the longer we wait to pursue our financial goals, the harder they become to reach. You have heard the saying, "The best time to plant a tree was 30 years ago. The next best time is today." If we started saving for retirement the day we were born, that would have been ideal. The next best time is today.

The same is true for you and I. We want to live for today and enjoy ourselves, and we want to make decisions to ensure a great life for our future-selves. There is a lot of value in taking a businesslike approach to our personal finances and our time-horizon planning. My goal is to give you the tools and ideas to make that happen in your life.

Fundamentally, you and I need money today. We will need it 10 years from now, and we will need it 30 years from now. Time horizon plays a critical role in planning our personal finances.

For personal finances, I break time horizon out like this:

- Short-term: Zero to three years
- Mid-term: Three to 10 years
- Long-term: 10+ years

## Short-term time horizon

Cash is an essential part of financial success. Businesses rely on their cash flow to meet obligations, and you and I need it to pay our bills and fund our lives. But how much?

The vast majority of Americans have less than $1,000 in savings, and almost half have $0.

The first step in securing your financial life is to get $1,000 saved up in your emergency fund. This should be in cash and should be in an account that's separate from your everyday checking account (a savings account works great). $1,000 is enough to cover most minor emergencies.

From there, your goal should be to save six months' worth of expenses.

I know that's a lot of money. And I know it will be hard to accumulate that much. But I also know once you do it, you will have financial peace of mind.

Once you've got your fully-funded emergency fund, resist the urge to invest the money. You should keep it in cash. The last thing I want is for you to experience an emergency and to discover your fund has decreased by 30% because the market went down.

Other short-term priorities include an annual vacation and getting out of debt.

## Mid-term time horizon

Your mid-term time horizon is three to ten years. Common priorities and goals are:

- Saving a down payment for a home
- Saving for a child's education
- Purchasing investment real estate
- Establishing and growing an investment portfolio
- Starting a business

### Long-term time horizon

Your long-term time horizon is 10+ years. Common priorities and goals are:

- Saving for retirement
- Estate planning and legacy desires
- Business succession planning

It's challenging to make sacrifices today in the service of saving for our abstract future selves. God-willing, we will all be old one day. And that older version of you will be grateful for your sacrifices.

**KEY TAKEAWAY**

Keeping your time horizon top of mind is an essential component to your financial plan.

**CALL TO ACTION**

Determine the time horizon for your financial goals and objectives.

# Chapter 14
# Saving and Investing

> ***CFO Best Practice**: It's a CFO's job to invest corporate assets (or decide not to). They must manage today's financial needs and the company's future needs. They're constantly working to maximize efficiency, profitability, and long-term value. Where's the best place to invest corporate assets? Where are they most needed? What can we afford to do? What can we afford not to do? These are just some questions CFOs must answer.*
>
> *For a CFO, cash can be as important as profit. Without cash, business operations won't be able to continue.*
>
> *When startups fail, liquidity is often the primary cause; meaning, they run out of cash. For more established businesses, as the costs to recruit and retain top talent increase, cash management becomes more important. Outside influences, such as inflation, can increase costs, adding additional pressure on cash management.*

Each of us must balance our immediate financial needs with our future needs. It's essential to prioritize how and where to save and invest our money.

Businesses begin as startups, continue through the growth stage, then on to maturity, and finally renewal or decline. We're all unique individuals, but we go through the same three stages of our financial lives. The first is protection, the second is accumulation, and the third is distribution.

Saving and investing money are critical to our financial success. And there are a lot of moving parts to do it. My focus is going to be on stock market investing, but there are certainly other opportunities to build wealth like real estate and investing in businesses.

## Your risk profile

Risk is the likelihood the investment you make gets the return you expect. For example, if you are expecting a 5% rate of return, what's the likelihood of getting it?

Informed by your risk tolerance, your investor profile seeks to help you determine your asset allocation. If you are okay with risk, you will have a more aggressive investor profile. If you are averse to risk, you will have a more conservative investor profile.

There are five traditional profiles:

1. Conservative
2. Moderate Conservative
3. Moderate
4. Moderate Aggressive
5. Aggressive

Your profile can remain static throughout your life or it can change. It can adjust as you get older, and/or it can adjust as you learn more about investing and have more experience.

Simply getting to know more about what kind of investor you are is a really important starting point.

## What kind of investor are you?

How do I know what kind of investor I am and what my risk tolerance is? You will need to complete a risk-tolerance profile.

You can find and download our Risk Profile worksheet at MoneyAlignmentAcademy.com/resources

Your profile will help you determine your asset allocation.

## Understanding asset allocation

Asset allocation is the term used to describe the investments (i.e., asset classes) you own. Often, an asset allocation will be created based on your answers from your risk-tolerance profile.

A common asset allocation is a 60/40 allocation, meaning 60% of your investable assets are equities (stocks) and 40% are fixed income (bonds). Your specific asset allocation should be contingent upon many variables such as age, time horizon, and risk tolerance.

Here's another example:

- 40% Stocks
- 20% Real estate
- 20% Cryptocurrency
- 10% Bonds
- 10% Cash

## Asset classes

Asset classes are groupings of similar investments.

- Equities (stocks, stock mutual funds, stock ETFs)
- Fixed income (bonds, bond mutual funds, bond ETFs)
- Cash and cash equivalents (checking, savings, money market accounts)
- Real estate (primary residence, investment real estate)
- Commodities (precious metals, oil, etc)
- Currencies (traditional)
- Art

- Private businesses
- Crypto assets (cryptocurrency, NFTs)

## Saving money

For a business, revenue - costs = profits. For individuals, earning - spending = savings. Saving is your ability to have money left over after you have paid all of your bills and made all of your expenditures.

Businesses and individuals must always have enough cash to meet immediate needs and expenses. Everyone has to pay their bills.

How much cash on hand you have is up to you. My recommendation is to have at least six months' worth of expenses saved in your emergency fund. That amount gives me financial peace of mind. You will need to make that decision for yourself and your situation.

## Cash on hand

Just as cash is paramount for businesses, it's the same for individuals and families. Everybody needs cash, but Americans are failing in this area. As I've already covered, the current state of savings for most Americans is dire.

We don't control what happens to us, only how we position ourselves and how we respond to adversity. Having enough cash on hand positions us to withstand emergencies. Failure to prepare leaves us extremely vulnerable.

## How much cash on hand should you have?

I mentioned at the beginning that it's a rule of thumb for both businesses and individuals to have at least three to six months' worth of expenses in cash. What do you think about that? Is that too much? Is that not enough?

It intellectually makes sense, but only 5% of Americans have between $10,000 and $20,000 in savings. How much do you currently have? How much would you like to have?

Big picture — I want you to become wildly financially successful. I want you to have whatever you want in life. But that will never happen unless you first find financial security. You get financial security by saving up six months' worth of expenses.

My perspective on this has changed from pre-pandemic to post-pandemic. I used to think three months was good enough. Today, I encourage everyone to get to six months. Once you get that saved up, you will have financial peace of mind. And that's one of the most valuable things you can ever have.

I'd like you to commit to making that happen in your life.

So how do you get there? Before I go any further, know this — it won't be easy. Six months' worth of expenses is a lot of money. There's a good chance you've never saved that much money before. Because of that, you will need to get focused and create a plan for making it happen.

## Getting to six months of cash on hand

Once you've gone through the review of your cash flow and created your budget, you will know how much your monthly expenses are. From there, you can put your plan together to save the money. For example, let's assume your monthly expenses are $3,000. Therefore, you will need to save $18,000 (6 x $3,000).

The reason I encourage you to think about your goals and your values is that you may need to make sacrifices to save that much money. And sacrificing for the sake of making sacrifices isn't compelling enough to do it. Instead, link any sacrifices to your most important financial goals and objectives. That will make difficult changes less difficult.

If you'd like to get your emergency complete in 12 months, you will need to be saving $1,500 a month. To do it in 24 months, you will need to save $750 a month. And to do it in 36 months, you will need to save $500 a month.

This is worth doing. It will be hard, but you can do hard things.

## Cash versus credit

Resist the impulse to rely on credit cards as your emergency fund. The harsh reality of poor economic times is that banks often reduce credit limits. If you've currently got a credit limit of $10,000, and the bank slashes it to $2,000, you'd be in big trouble if that was your emergency fund.

Your emergency fund must be cash on hand.

Also, resist the impulse to invest the money. I know that it may be tempting. However, the last thing I want is for you to need the money, only to have it reduced due to market fluctuations.

This is worth doing. It will be hard, but you can do hard things.

## Investing money

Investing is buying assets that increase in value and provide a return. To reach our financial goals and objectives, investing our money is required.

The major difference between investing and speculating is the amount of risk. Speculation can be thought of like gambling, whereas investing is based on research and the known fundamentals of the asset you are putting money towards.

It's useful to consider your time horizon when deciding what and where to invest. If your savings/investing objective will happen within three years, it's prudent to have your money invested in cash or a very conservative investment. No one knows what the stock market will do tomorrow, and you don't want your money at risk.

## Time horizon

Your short-term time horizon is zero to three years. Mid-term is three to 10 years, and long-term is 10+ years.

## Asset location

We talked about asset allocation (your investment mix), and it's also important to understand asset location. Simply put, it's where you hold the investments. Common examples are bank accounts, brokerage accounts, and qualified accounts. Because we've already covered bank accounts, I will focus on brokerage and qualified accounts here.

## Qualified accounts

Just as a CFO works to maximize efficiency, profitability, and long-term value, individuals must also do the same. Keeping your goals and values top of mind as you make savings and investing decisions is an important starting point. From there, you must know what kind of investor you are and how comfortable you are with risk. Next, make good decisions about your asset allocation, as well as your asset location.

While thinking about it in total can feel intimidating and confusing, taking it step-by-step will help you find success. Taking a business-like approach to your personal finances will help get you where you want to go.

In 1875, the American Express Company developed the first private pension in the United States. Before that, the military and government had been providing pensions since 1781. In 1935, Social Security was introduced and it evolved throughout the century.

In 1978, the 401(k) was born. This qualified account grew in popularity and today, it's replaced pensions as the primary vehicle Americans use to save for retirement.

A pension is a type of defined benefit plan. 401(k)s are a type of defined contribution account. Defined benefit plans specify the amount of benefit (income) the participant will receive. Defined contributions plans specify only how much employers will contribute to the plan (if anything).

One of the key differences is this — the bulk of responsibility for retirement security has shifted to me and you. We are responsible for saving and investing enough money to one day move away from full-time employment and into retirement.

Unfortunately, many Americans have neither accepted nor embraced that responsibility. The average American doesn't have enough saved for retirement.

***The benefits of qualified accounts***

There are a lot of benefits to qualified accounts, ranging from tax benefits to potential employer contributions. Einstein famously called compound interest the eighth wonder of the world, and every type of qualified account provides this.

Contributions can also be automated. This helps you to pay yourself first, which is the Golden Rule of personal finance. If you are fortunate to work at a company that offers a 401(k), you can elect to have contributions deducted from your pay before they hit your bank account. You can also accomplish this by opening an IRA and setting up automatic contributions at the beginning of each month.

In the absence of pensions, qualified accounts are your best option to prepare for retirement.

### ***Types and rules around qualified accounts***

There are a lot of different qualified accounts. IRAs, Roth IRAs, 401(k)s, 403(b)s, SEP IRAs, and SIMPLE IRAs are the most common qualified accounts. Some accounts, like the 401(k), can only be offered by employers. Others, like IRAs, can be opened by anyone with earned income.

There are a lot of rules around qualified accounts. It's important to educate yourself on them and to recognize things like contribution amounts can change yearly. Here are the key areas to be aware of:

- **Contribution amounts**: There are limits to how much money you can contribute to qualified accounts each year. The IRS has a lot of helpful resources to stay up to date.

- **Time horizon**: These are designed for long-term savings, specifically for retirement. With some exceptions, you are not supposed to take money out of these accounts before you turn 59 and a half.

- **Investment options**: Within 401(k)s, the most common investment options are mutual funds and ETFs. IRAs offer more flexibility and allow for most any type of investment.

Though not overly complicated, it's important to stay up-to-date with the rules for qualified accounts.

### ***How to think about qualified accounts***

Unless you are working for the government, military, or are fortunate enough to have a pension at your company, your qualified account is your go-to place for saving for retirement.

Thinking about ourselves getting old is an abstract thing, but God-willing, we will all be old one day. With that in mind, we need to be putting money away for our future-selves. You've heard the saying, "The best time to plant a tree was 30 years ago. The next best time is today." And certainly, if you'd started saving for retirement at 15, you'd be much better off than if you waited until 55. Either way now is the time to be saving and investing for retirement.

While investing in individual stocks is tempting, a diversified approach is the best approach to investing for retirement. You accomplish this through mutual funds and ETFs. It's also important to pay attention to the fees and expenses of your investments and your investment accounts. You can learn about the expenses inside your 401(k) by obtaining the fee disclosure statement, and about the expenses of the investments themselves from the prospectus.

The earlier you start, the better. Even if you are contributing 1% of your income every month, you will be developing a positive habit.

***Roth versus traditional contributions***

Is it better to make Roth or traditional contributions to your qualified account? It depends. Here's the difference, and a simple way to think about it.

You can make a Roth or traditional contribution (also known as pre-tax) to your 401(k), and you can open a Roth or traditional IRA.

When you make a traditional (pre-tax) contribution, you are reducing your earned income for that income tax year, which could result in a lower income tax liability. What that means is that you will pay income tax on ***ALL*** the money when you withdraw it (both principal and interest).

When you make a Roth contribution, you are not reducing your earned income for that income tax year, so you are not lowering your income tax liability. When you withdraw the money down the road, you get to take out the money income tax free (both principal and interest).

In summary, if you want to reduce your current year's income tax liability, making a traditional contribution could make sense. If you'd like to have all your retirement income tax-free, making Roth-style contributions could make sense.

## Brokerage accounts

Also known as taxable accounts, a brokerage account allows you to buy and sell securities such as stocks, bonds, ETFs (exchange-traded funds), mutual funds, and crypto assets. Common examples are Charles Schwab, Fidelity, and ETrade. You may also be familiar with upstarts, Robinhood and Acorns.

Key differences between brokerage accounts and qualified accounts include, but aren't limited to:

- There are no contribution limits placed on brokerage accounts. You can put as much money into these accounts as you want.
- There are no time horizon limitations on brokerage accounts. You can withdraw funds from your account before 59 and a half.
- You don't enjoy the same tax benefits with a brokerage account that you do with a qualified account. With brokerage accounts, there are no tax deductions on contributions or tax-deferred growth.

## How much to save?

You should save as much as you can. No one ever got to retirement and said, "I wish I hadn't saved all this money."

In all seriousness, I encourage you to try to accumulate $1,000,000 for your retirement. Doing so will position you for long-term financial success.

Even if you end up coming up short, it's far better to plan big and fall short than to plan small (or not plan at all) and, as a result, have little to no money left for retirement.

**KEY TAKEAWAY**

Accumulating an emergency fund of six months' of expenses will provide financial peace of mind.

**CALL TO ACTION**

Decide out how much your emergency fund should be and how long it will take to save it.

# Chapter 15
# Staying on Top of Your Finances

***CFO Best Practice***: *CFOs handle the finances of their organizations, and many stakeholders rely on their data and insight. They look back at historical results, as well as plan and forecast for the future. The rest of the executive team, as well as shareholders, look to them for guidance on the company's financial future.*

*CFOs accomplish this by reviewing cash flow statements, balance sheets, and income statements. This information is critical in the planning process; without accurate data, there's no way of knowing if an idea makes financial sense.*

In personal finance as well as corporate, what gets measured, gets managed.

To be positioned for financial success, individuals and families engage in a similar process. They must look back and review financial information, evaluate the results, and make any necessary changes moving forward.

For optimal success, organizations and families must communicate consistently and openly. Being on the same page with money is without question a best practice.

I've already detailed the common financial struggles of many Americans, and those realities are a problem. When something is a problem, creating a system can help alleviate the challenge moving forward.

Many people don't know how to fix their financial problems. Others are aware but choose not to do what's required to move past those problems. Too often, people wait until their financial problems get too big to ignore, or they hit rock bottom. In reality, the total work required to create and maintain good financial systems is far less than picking yourself up from rock bottom.

## Reviewing your finances

To create a system to stay on top of your personal finances, you need to track the correct financial information. You must track your cash flow so you know this important equation: income - expenses = savings.

You must maintain a personal balance sheet so you can look at all of your account balances in one place. It's important to track your bank account balances, investment accounts, retirement accounts, and any other financial accounts.

It's essential to maintain a personal budget, and you must track and review it.

Finally, you need to review the status of your most important financial goals and priorities.

It's prudent to create an agenda or checklist of all the items you will review during your planning meeting.

## Evaluating the results

Mike Tyson famously said, "Everyone has a plan until they get punched in the mouth." While he was referring to his fight with Evander Holyfield, it's true for me and you as well. Planning positions us for success, but after that, we have to let the chips fall where they may.

Every time you review your finances, you are looking at how your plan stood up to reality. Did you execute your plans? Did you save and invest as much as you planned to? From there, what were the actual results? Did the markets perform as you expected?

In every area that you are tracking, determine if your behaviors and planning met your expectations.

## Making necessary changes

Money has time value (meaning the longer we wait, the harder reaching our financial goals becomes), so the sooner we can make changes, the better off we are.

Rarely will everything work out exactly as you had planned. This is to be expected, so don't get frustrated. Rather, look for opportunities to optimize and change your planning process and behaviors.

Balancing short-term and long-term financial goals and priorities isn't an easy thing. When your results aren't what you planned for, it can be tempting to make big changes. While major changes are sometimes required, it's important to maintain perspective.

This is particularly true regarding the stock market. Over the long-term, the stock market has consistently gone up. Over the short-term, the stock market fluctuates daily. When the market has a correction (i.e., when it goes down by 20% or more), it's natural to want to sell your investments. But in actuality, all that does is guarantee your loss. Instead of selling, maintain your long-term strategy and continue to consistently review your approach.

All of this assumes you've taken the time to determine your risk profile, create an appropriate asset allocation, and select high-quality investments.

## Identifying and involving your stakeholders

You will need to decide how much of your finances to share, but there are a lot of benefits to involving loved ones in your review and planning process.

The more you can normalize talking about money, the more comfortable loved ones (particularly children) will be with the topic. When you talk about money with others, their level of financial literacy will increase. This will help them become financially successful.

It's also true that people support what they help to create. When you involve loved ones in your planning process, it will get them engaged and encourage them to take ownership. Involving them in planning and decision-making is nothing but a positive thing.

## How often to conduct your reviews

As you are getting started, I encourage you to conduct your financial reviews every month. Once you are in the habit of doing them and get on track to meeting your financial goals and objectives, you can switch to quarterly reviews.

You must put these meetings in your calendar. The last thing I want is for you to forget or ignore these meetings. When you schedule a meeting, it makes it more important. And financial planning is definitely important.

When you create and follow your financial review and planning process, you position yourself for long-term success. Taking a businesslike approach to managing your personal finances will greatly benefit you.

**KEY TAKEAWAY**

Review your finances on a monthly basis.

**CALL TO ACTION**

Decide what day and time you'll review your finances every month.

# Chapter 16
# Automating Your Finances

*__CFO Best Practice__: CFOs are always interested in optimizing and reducing time spent on menial tasks. Automation of functions like payroll, invoicing, expense management, and bookkeeping allows finance teams to spend more time focused on the big picture. Technology has made it possible to devote more resources to forecasting, solving client problems, and adding value to more areas within the organization.*

Is it possible to "set it and forget it" with our personal finances?

Our time and attention are just as valuable as our money. When we can stop doing menial tasks like paying bills and balancing our checkbooks, we can spend our time and attention on other things. And, when we can take our hands off the wheel, we remove the possibility of human error, which can cause unnecessary fees.

Technology has made it possible to automate many aspects of our financial lives. While it's true that we don't have to spend as much time as we used to, it's still imperative we pay close attention to our money.

**The starting point**

All the technology in the world won't replace the need for planning. In order to get where you want to go with your money, you need to have a coherent plan. Once you've set your goals and objectives and you know what it will take to reach them, automating as much as possible makes sense.

## Set your goals and objectives

I like to think about goal setting in terms of time horizon. You need money today, you will need it in five years, as well as 30 years from now. Short-term is considered zero to three years, mid-term three to 10, and long-term is 10+.

## Open, or enroll in, the appropriate accounts

Once you know what you want to accomplish, it's time to enroll in, or open, the appropriate accounts. For short-term goals, you will need checking and savings accounts. For mid-term goals, you will need taxable brokerage accounts. Finally, for long-term goals, you will need qualified accounts like your 401(k) at work, or a traditional or Roth IRA.

Now it's time to set it and forget it.

## Automating menial tasks

A menial task does not require much skill. Examples of menial financial tasks are paying bills and balancing bank accounts. Here are some areas where it's easy to create automation.

### *Direct deposit*

Odds are that you are already receiving your paycheck via direct deposit. If you are still receiving paper checks in the mail, work to get those payments directly deposited into your checking account.

### *Automatic bill pay*

Slowly but surely, we're moving away from writing checks and putting stamps on envelopes to pay our bills. Setting up automatic bill pay through your bank will save you a lot of time.

### *Email notifications*

When you can't automate a payment, ask for (or create your own) email reminder. Without a reminder, it's easy to let things slip through the cracks.

## Online banking and account management

Online banking has made balancing our checkbooks obsolete. Take advantage of online access to all your financial accounts.

## Recurring calendar events

Just because our lives are moving online doesn't mean you no longer need to schedule a time to review your finances. I encourage you to schedule a monthly meeting to review your finances. Below are the items to include in your review.

- Your cash flow
- Your budget
- Your goals and objectives
- Your progress toward those goals and objectives.

Creating a recurring monthly meeting on the same day and time helps ensure you won't skip this important meeting (e.g., the first Sunday of every month at 8 pm).

## Proactive automation

Automating menial tasks is great, and there are also opportunities to use automation more proactively.

### *Pay yourself first*

The Golden Rule of personal finance is, "Pay yourself first." This means you are contributing to your personal financial goals before paying anyone else. You can accomplish this in several ways:

- Set up automatic contributions or transfers from your checking account to a savings account.
- Enroll in your company's 401(k) and set up automatic contributions.
- Set up automatic contributions to a taxable brokerage account, IRA, or 529 plan.

***Automated investing***

Technology has made sophisticated investing available to everyone. Mutual funds and ETFs have made diversification simple. Roboadvisors have made rebalancing our portfolios and tax-loss harvesting automatic.

Once we are clear on our priorities, it's possible to set and forget many aspects of our personal financial lives.

Get clear on your biggest financial goals and objectives. Create plans for accomplishing them. Open the accounts for completing them. Set your plans in motion by automating as many of the menial tasks as possible.

While it's extremely valuable to automate menial tasks and to take our hands off the figurative wheel, we need to maintain complete ownership of our finances. Scheduling and completing a monthly review of your personal finances will position you for long-term financial success.

**KEY TAKEAWAY**

Automate as many menial financial tasks as you can.

**CALL TO ACTION**

Determine which aspects of your financial life you can automate and make it happen.

# Chapter 17
# The Human Element

***CFO Best Practice**: In business, it's impossible to avoid making bad decisions. The idea is to make as few of them as possible. CFOs are trained to be objective and logical. They take a long-term perspective on decision-making, taking into consideration the past, present, and future. Because they are constantly balancing competing interests, they have an acute understanding of tradeoffs.*

*Recognizing that humans don't always make rational decisions or have all of the information necessary to make a decision, the CFO will collaborate with others in the organization. They recognize everyone has blindspots and biases, and another set of eyes can be valuable.*

We all want to know how to be good at financial decision-making. And it's easy, but it's not simple.

The reality is that no one can eliminate all bad decisions. What we want to do is minimize how many we make. The wrong financial decision can delay our most important financial goals.

Being human is to be both logical and emotional. We can understand something intellectually but still act emotionally.

Over my life, there have been a lot of things I intellectually understood but didn't do.

While I'm getting better, I still have to learn certain things for myself instead of relying on the wisdom and experiences of others.

The gap between knowing and doing has been consistently closing for me as I've gotten older, but I have a feeling it's always going to be there in some form. And that's okay though because I'm aware of it.

For me, behavioral finance is all about becoming aware of that gap as it relates to our money. Awareness is the first step in closing it.

A technical definition of behavioral finance is this from Kaplan:

> "Behavioral finance is the study of the effects of psychology on investors and financial markets. It focuses on explaining why investors often appear to lack self-control, act against their own best interest, and make decisions based on personal biases instead of facts."

Our brains are awesome tools and, for the most part, they benefit us greatly. But, they're not necessarily serving us when it comes to our finances.

Having a better understanding of behavioral finance and how it applies in your life will help you get better at money which will result in a better and richer life.

### Ideal versus real

If we lived in an ideal world, there would be ideal scenarios.

But we don't, so there's not.

The same is true for our finances. We don't live inside a spreadsheet, so our finances are never going to play out perfectly. And that's okay.

We need to know ourselves and our brains, so we can do a better job of getting to where we want to go. We need to be as real with ourselves as we possibly can and not sugarcoat things.

We have all made mistakes, and we will make more in the future. As we become more aware of our mistakes and our reasons for making them, we become more likely to avoid them.

To do this, we need to understand how our brains operate.

## Our brains and money

"This is your brain. This is drugs. This is your brain on drugs. Any questions?"

Do you remember that 1987 anti-drug TV commercial? If you don't, do yourself a favor and check it out on YouTube.

Our brains are amazing. They have kept humanity going for six million years. But, they're not awesome at money.

What percentage of your financial decisions do you make emotionally?

Nobel Prize-winning Economist and Psychologist Daniel Kahneman figured out it's around 90%.

What do you think about that?

I was taken aback the first time I heard it. I thought, "No way. There's no way I make 90% of my financial decisions emotionally."

But then I thought about it.

And the more I thought about it, the more I started believing it. Once you start to pay attention to how you think about and make financial decisions, you will be able to stop making financial decisions based on your emotion. And that's what we want.

Here's another interesting fact — the part of our brain that handles our finances is the same part that handles mortal danger. So the feelings and responses we get when we smell smoke, are the same as when we check our 401(k) balance and see it's declined 20%. Our brains tell us to RUN!

In terms of escaping a burning building, the response is extremely helpful. But when it comes to our investments, we can't run away without risking our livelihoods.

You see, I intellectually understand I'm supposed to buy low and sell high. But my brain wants me to do the opposite.

When it sees my investments have gone down, it tells me to sell.

Conversely, when it sees an investment at an all-time high, it tells us to buy. Our brains want us to avoid pain and to find pleasure. This is often the opposite of successful financial behavior.

## Common biases

We've all got biases and blindspots. Becoming aware of and spotting them when they're happening is how we overcome them.

Here are the most common biases and how they show themselves.

- **Self-attribution b**ias: Our egos love taking credit when things go right and redirecting blame when things go wrong. We also tend to believe ourselves to be more competent than we actually are.
- **Confirmation bias**: We do this all the time. In the context of finance, we seek information to confirm our existing beliefs or hypothesis.
- **Representative b**ias: We make this mistake by comparing one investment to another we consider to be similar, but may have a completely different set of facts.

- **Framing bias**: This happens when we make poor decisions based on how something is presented, instead of judging on merits alone.

- **Anchoring bias**: We put too much faith in the first piece of information we receive. Instead of looking at new information objectively, we allow it to be influenced by the initial info.

- **Loss aversion**: The pain of loss is said to be twice as powerful as the desire for gain. This fear often causes investors to hold onto bad investments for far too long.

## Overcoming our biases

Success with behavioral finance means becoming aware that there's a gap between what we know and what we do. Awareness is the first step in closing it.

Learning about the various biases that exist is the starting point. Next, we need to become more mindful and recognize when we are experiencing them. From there, it's having the discipline to make logical decisions instead of emotional ones.

It's also wise to have someone with whom you can share your thoughts and ideas. When we are facing an important financial decision, being able to talk it through with someone else can be valuable. If you have a partner, it can be this person. If that's not available, find a trusted friend with whom you can have this serious conversation. Working with a financial professional could also be a solution to this problem.

Embracing the logical and emotional parts of ourselves is essential. We will never get rid of emotions in our decision-making process. Therefore, we need to become adept at managing it.

Financial success requires paying attention to your thinking and behavior around money. It requires being aware of things like behavioral finance.

It's hard to develop new habits, but easier to keep them going. Like all muscles, as you use and exercise it, it gets stronger.

Having a better understanding of behavioral finance and how it applies in your life will help you get better at money, which will result in a better and richer life.

**KEY TAKEAWAY**

Optimize your financial decision-making by recognizing how our brains work.

**CALL TO ACTION**

Think and write about any financial blind spots or biases you may fall victim to.

# Chapter 18
# Delegating

***CFO Best Practice**: We've spent a lot of time talking about the importance of the CFO to an organization, and how they perform the many important tasks which fall under their purview. But that doesn't mean they do all of them. The best CFOs are also adept at delegation.*

*To maximize your financial potential, you need to determine which aspects of your personal finances you are interested in and willing to do, and what aspects you are not interested in or willing to do. Whatever you are not going to do still needs to get done. That's where delegation comes in.*

Being your own CFO doesn't mean you need to do everything relating to your personal finances. It does mean you need to make sure everything gets done.

It's really important to be honest with yourself about which aspects of your finances you are interested in doing and which aspects you are not. And there's no right or wrong answer.

Thinking about your financial plan as though you are building a house is an appropriate analogy. If you intend to do your own planning, you will take on the most important role — the general contractor.

As with any project, there has to be someone whose job it is to get everything done — to understand what the overall plan is, and to ensure all of the subcontractors (Accounts, vehicles, legal documents) are doing their jobs.

A good general contractor has the experience and expertise, and can make the project run more smoothly.

If you find you need additional help, I want to share some thoughts on how best to engage with professionals.

## The different types of financial professionals

There are upwards of 300,000 people working in personal finance. There are over 200,000 financial advisors.

When you think of a financial advisor, what comes to mind? Is it a buttoned-up professional in a big office? That's what I think of, and there are certainly a lot of professionals who fit that description. But many do not. Here are some of the different kinds of financial professionals.

***Financial planners***

A financial planner helps you create and implement a financial plan. They are trained to help you get clear on your financial goals and objectives, and then put plans together to help you reach them. They have a working knowledge of many aspects of personal finance.

***Investment advisors***

An investment advisor's job is to help you with your investments. They're trained to help you determine your risk tolerance, financial objectives, create an asset allocation, and help you to make investment decisions.

***Financial services professionals***

A financial services professional may represent a specific company, or they may work as a broker of several companies. They may assist with you one aspect of your financial situation like insurance, or they may take a more comprehensive approach.

### *Financial coaches*

Financial coaches are a relatively new type of professional. They focus more on helping their clients with their financial behaviors and habits. They don't provide advice or sell products.

### *FinTech options*

FinTech (Financial Technology) companies are technology-enabled. Larger companies wish to cater to and help ordinary investors by offering investment advice through something called a "robo-advisor." Robo-advisors are low-cost investment managers who utilize software to make investment decisions. Oftentimes, clients of a robo-advisor will have access to dedicated financial professionals who can answer questions.

As the financial services industry continues to grow and evolve, I think consumers will continue to benefit. That being said, it can be confusing to determine what type of professional you need. Having the right questions to ask will help you find the appropriate professional for your situation.

## The best questions to ask a financial advisor

Going through the different kinds of professionals, you no doubt have a lot of questions. If you are serious about engaging with a professional, it's really important to be crystal clear about everyone's expectations. The more work you can do on the front end, the better off you will be.

Here are the best questions to ask:

### *How are you compensated?*

Many people are uncomfortable asking others how they're paid. I sure used to be. But this is one of the most important questions you need to ask. It will tell you a lot more than the dollar amount. This question will help you determine their motivations for the recommendations that they are giving you (i.e., Are they product or commission driven?).

Also, if they are not comfortable or unable to answer this question, that's a bit red flag and you should not engage with them.

Some professionals will earn a commission from the sale of products. Some will earn a percentage of the assets you have invested with them. Some will charge you a flat fee for creating a financial, some will charge you based on the hour, and some will charge an annual fee.

Will you, the client, be paying them? Or will another financial company be paying them?

***What kind of work do you do?***
You need to know what kind of professional they are. Will they help you create an entire financial plan? Will they help you with your 401(k)? It's essential to know their scope of services and what you should expect.

***Can I see your work product?***
They should have a "finished product" their clients receive. It could simply be a PDF document that reflects your financial goals and the strategies for achieving them, but it's important to ask what you will get from working with them.

***What data will you need from me and how will you analyze it?***
Will you need investment account information, tax returns, insurance policies, legal documents, goals, and objectives? The data and information the professional requests will help you to better understand if they're going to take a holistic look at your finances or focus on specific areas.

***What products do you sell?***
They may not sell any financial products at all, or they may sell many financial products like insurance policies, annuities, or investments. You must know the full scope of the work they do.

***What do you do when your clients need a product you don't sell?***
If they don't sell products you want/need, will they introduce you to another professional who can help you?

***What does a successful client relationship look like for you?***
This question involves things like:

- How do they interact with clients?
- What are their expectations of their clients?
- What will our relationship look like?
- How often will we meet/communicate?
- What if I have a question?
- Can you call or email them anytime you like?
- How often can you meet with them?

***Are you a fiduciary?***
Being a fiduciary means you are legally obligated to act in your client's best interest. When hiring a financial advisor, investment advisor, or financial planner, I think working with a fiduciary is essential. There are enough of them out there and there are no reasons to work with someone who is not.

**Asking the questions**

This is certainly something you can email to them in advance of meeting with them. Simply say this, "I'm looking forward to our conversation. Please take a look at this list of questions I'd like to cover during our time together."

**How to find your financial professional**

I think the best way to meet anyone is through a referral or personal introduction. Ask someone you like and trust who they work with, and ask them to make an introduction.

**How will you gain the information and knowledge you need?**

We all have biases and blindspots. We're carrying a lot of baggage around with us. Working with a professional can help us avoid missteps.

The reality is that the world of personal finance is immense. There's investing, insurance, tax, and estate planning to name a few. There aren't too many of us that have a high level of literacy in every area.

You can certainly learn it on your own.

For example, if you lack literacy in investing, you could read blog posts, listen to podcasts, read a book, take a course, or work with an advisor or a coach.

For example, if you are experiencing gaps in your planning, you will need to learn more about creating a cohesive plan. You can do this through personal research or through engaging with a coach or an advisor.

Overcoming what's holding you back may require resources.

Where can you get the new knowledge you need? Knowing where you can go for information and knowledge is extremely important.

Do you want to spend time on this?

Some people really enjoy personal finance and investing, while others would prefer to not spend much time on it. There's no right or wrong answer to this question. Again, it's important to be honest with yourself.

Will you spearhead this effort, or will you find partners?

These are the questions you need to answer. If you are not going to do it, then it may be important to find someone to work with.

## Three models for achieving financial success

Whether you are trying to get better at personal finance, relationships, or leadership skills, there are three models for doing it.

1. **DIY Model**. Information and raw data are everywhere. I've certainly combed through it all to learn new skills. You can listen to podcasts, watch YouTube videos, and read blogs on literally every topic. The information on personal finance is no different.

2. **Invest Model**. Tapping into the knowledge and teachings of others can greatly enhance the learning process. I have paid for and benefitted from many courses from college to online learning. There are a lot of courses for improving your finances.

3. **Partner Model**. Wisdom is more valuable today than ever. Getting the support and expertise from a coach, advisor, or mastermind can get you where you want to go a lot faster. Working with a financial advisor, a financial coach, or collaborating with a mastermind can help you get where you want to go a lot faster.

Obviously, the more you can interact with an expert, the better. But if you have the time and attention, you can most certainly piece everything together on your own.

**KEY TAKEAWAY**

As the CFO of you, you need to make sure everything gets done. Whatever you are not going to do, you need to find people to get it done. From there, you trust but verify. That means you vet them, allow them to do their jobs, and review their work to ensure proper completion.

**CALL TO ACTION**

Think and write about whether or not you would benefit from working with a financial professional.

# Chapter 19
# Accountability

---

> ***CFO Best Practice**: Money touches every aspect of a business. As the corporate officer in charge of the organization's finances, the CFO must ensure everyone who reports to them is doing their job. Because of that, they must possess strong leadership and communication skills and be able to hold all other stakeholders accountable.*

What is the importance of accountability with your money? Since money plays a vital role in every aspect of our lives, accountability is critical. We must hold ourselves, our loved ones, and our partners accountable.

Another important consideration is the time value of money. Meaning, the longer we wait to pursue a financial goal, the harder it becomes to reach. It's a very human thing to put things off until "tomorrow." Unfortunately for many of us, "tomorrow" becomes next year, the year after, and sometimes never. Procrastination keeps us from accomplishing many financial goals.

To break free from procrastination, give yourself short deadlines and high expectations. Once you've done that, be accountable for making them happen. I'm going to give you the tools necessary for making that happen.

## The key areas of financial accountability

There are five key areas where financial accountability is required — earning, spending, saving, investing, and giving.

***1. Earning***

To plan properly, you need to project how much money you are going to earn each year. Along the way, you need to check your progress every month. This may be easier if you have a salaried W2 career and more difficult if you have a variable income. Either way, set an earnings number that will allow you to plan and budget.

***2. Spending***

It's essential to hold all parties accountable for their spending. To be financially successful, you must keep a budget and track your cash flow (i.e., income and expenses). Monitoring this monthly will allow you to make any necessary adjustments.

***3. Saving***

To meet your financial objectives, all stakeholders need to agree on the savings goals. Monitoring your progress monthly will help you know if you are on track.

***4. Investing***

To meet your mid and long-term financial goals, you will need to consistently invest your money. While we have little control over the stock market and our rate of return, we can be accountable for the amount we are investing.

***5. Giving***

If giving money is a priority for you, make sure you have goals set for how much and where you will give.

## Self-accountability

Is it possible to hold yourself accountable? Yes, but it's difficult. It will be difficult if you are not currently in the habit of doing it. Accountability is a skill that can be learned and improved upon. It's also like a muscle that will atrophy when it's not used.

Taking personal responsibility for your financial life is a key to your success, and an integral part of personal responsibility is accountability. You need to know what you want and need to do, then do the things that are required.

As you are building your accountability skill and muscle, be patient with yourself. You will not be great at it right away, but you will achieve mastery if you stick with it.

## Accountability partners

While I am a massive fan of personal responsibility and self-accountability, there's a lot of value to involving others. The research doesn't lie.

You are 65% more likely to meet a goal after committing to another person. If you establish an ongoing partnership, your chances increase to 95%. Those numbers are too powerful to ignore. An accountability partner can help you track your goals and call you out when needed if you are making excuses. They can be a sounding board should you run into a problem and can't figure it out on your own.

Who should you partner with?

Anyone in your household who earns or spends money, and any professionals who help you with your finances can be an accountability partners.

Your significant other should be involved in your accountability process and so should your children. This does not mean that your children need to know everything about your household finances, but as they get older, there is a lot of value to involving them in your planning and review process.

If you work with a financial advisor, tax professional, estate planner, or any other financial professional, they need to be involved in your accountability process. It's important to trust them and to also verify that they're doing great work on your behalf.

Let's talk about how to do it.

## The accountability process

Managing expectations is essential to happy and healthy relationships. This is true of your relationship with your romantic partner, family members, and business partners. Having a clear framework for managing expectations and holding one another accountable will help you be as successful as possible. There are five steps in this process:

1. **Be crystal clear in your expectations**. Doing this will help everyone avoid mutual mystification. It will remove guessing from the equation. Be clear with your partners about what you expect from them and what they can expect from you.

2. **Make sure your partners are competent**. Do your partners know how to do what you are asking them to do? If not, you need to help them learn or give the responsibility to someone else.

3. **Agree on how you will track progress**. When and how will you check in and report on what they have completed and the next steps?

4. **Embrace and expect dialogue**. Open, honest, and robust communication is essential. You should expect feedback from your partners, and they should expect it from you — good and bad.

5. **Be crystal clear on how results will be handled**. What will happen when goals are met? What will happen when they are not?

Money plays a critical role in every aspect of our lives. The more upfront and honest we can be with the stakeholders in our life, the better off we will be. Following this five-step process will help improve your relationships and increase your likelihood of success.

We are capable of a lot, so I think it's important to ask a lot of ourselves. This is why it's important to set high expectations. Because of the human tendency to procrastinate, we need to give ourselves deadlines.

That being said, I also don't want you to set such a high pace that you end up burning out. Start thinking about accountability as a muscle that you can train and strengthen. Then make a habit out of training that muscle every day.

Remember, this isn't a New Year's resolution that you give up on after one slip-up. Rather, you commit to making accountability a permanent fixture in your life. You can do this. You can do hard things.

**KEY TAKEAWAY**

We all benefit from having an accountability partner.

**CALL TO ACTION**

Who will your accountability partner be? When will you reach out to them?

# Chapter 20
# Closing

When will you take action on the ideas in this book? When will you respond to the calls to action?

I want to know what day and time you will do it.

What normally happens on that day and time? If there's something else occupying that spot on your calendar, that's not going to work. You must find a time where you will be able to dedicate 100% of your attention to this. Why? Because this is far too important not to.

The main idea of this book is that there will never be anyone more interested in your financial success than you. So, it's time to start acting accordingly.

The first step to success is accepting and embracing that reality. The second is creating your plan. The third step is putting that plan into action.

The longer you wait, the harder it becomes to reach your most important financial goals and objectives. Find a day and time that works, and get started. You are fully capable of becoming financially successful. Commit to it and get started.

Made in the USA
Middletown, DE
16 November 2022